Food and Drink France

AA Publishing

Globe artichokes reach for the sun in rural Brittany.

1

Original text by Hazel Evans

New text and updates by Fay Franklin

Produced by AA Publishing

© Automobile Association Developments Limited 2008

Map © Automobile Association Developments Limited 2008

Updated 2008

A CIP catalogue record for this book is available from the British Library.

ISBN 978-0-7495-5947-2

A03675

Automobile Association Developments Limited retains the copyright in the original edition © 2001 and in all
subsequent editions, reprints and amendments.

All rights reserved. No part of this publication may be reproduced, stored in a retrieval system, or transmitted in
any form or by any means – electronic, photocopying, recording or otherwise – unless the written permission
of the publishers has been obtained beforehand. This book may not be sold, resold, hired out or otherwise
disposed of by way of trade in any form of binding or cover other than that in which it is published, without the
prior consent of the publisher.

The contents of this publication are believed correct at the time of printing. Nevertheless, the publishers cannot
be held responsible for any errors or omissions or for changes in the details given in this guide or for the conse-
quences of any reliance on the information provided by the same. This does not affect your statutory rights.
Assessments are based upon the author's own experience and, therefore, descriptions given in this guide
necessarily contain an element of subjective opinion, which may not reflect the publisher's opinion or dictate
a reader's own experience on another occasion. We have tried to ensure accuracy in this guide, but things do
change and we would be grateful if readers would advise us of any inaccuracies they may encounter.

Published by AA Publishing, a trading name of Automobile Association Developments Limited, whose registered office is Fanum House, Basing View, Basingstoke, Hampshire RG21 4EA. Registered number 1878835.

Colour separation by Keenes, Andover, UK

Printed and bound in China by Everbest

Contents

About this Book

One of the pleasures of travelling is sampling the local food and drink. Whether your tastes are adventurous or conservative, this book will whet your appetite and give you a genuine taste of France. The perfect dining companion, it may change your ideas about what is on offer in this gourmet's paradise. As well as helping you to appreciate the true flavours of the country, it will take the worry out of unfamiliar situations and help you to order what you want. This book is organised into the following chapters:

Food of France
France's regions are colourfully described, with the emphasis on local foods and specialities, and a look at the influences and traditions you can still detect in them. A comprehensive A–Z covers the foods you are likely to see in shops and markets and the dishes that appear on menus.

Wine and Drink of France
Here you will find information and advice on wines and an A–Z of other drinks, both alcoholic and non-alcoholic.

Eating Out
The Eating Out section can help you decide where to eat and at what time. There are also tips on catering for children.

Eating In
The shopping guide offers advice on different types of shops, what you can buy and shopping for particular dietary requirements. The recipes include some of the most famous regional dishes and will appeal to cooks of all abilities.

Practical Information
This chapter contains essential information such as managing a tight budget and planning a self-catering holiday. A short section highlights festivals and holidays, and the types of food and drink that feature at these events. Understanding the menu can sometimes be a problem and there are handy phrases to use in a variety of shops and restaurants. Finally, there is a conversion table to help with the shopping.

Food of France

You will find olives of every size and colour for sale at the Saxe-Breteuil market in Paris.

Blue cheeses on display at the Marché Président Wilson in Paris.

Food of France

No other country has influenced inter-national cooking as much as France. It offers such a diversity of dishes that you need to return again and again just to sample the specialities on offer in each region.

Some of the meals served up are influenced by countries beyond the French borders, from the hearty Teutonic-style dishes of Alsace, leaning heavily on *choucroute*, (sauerkraut) to the Spanish influences that permeate the foods from the Basque country, and the Italian-inspired dishes from Nice. But having been influenced by a neighbouring food, the French will always add a touch that makes a dish entirely their own.

The culinary arts in France were advanced by the arrival of Catherine de' Medici at the French court for her marriage to Henri II in the 16th century and, like all courtly fashions, they spread from there down to the ordinary French people.

Louis XIV developed the custom of serving dishes in a particular order, and the French Revolution brought with it not only civil liberties, but also a higher standard of cooking for the masses, as the chefs of the (former) nobility found new employment by opening public dining rooms, or 'restaurants'.

French cuisine is, of course, noted for its delicious sauces, which enhance the texture and flavour of the food; herbs and spices are also widely used, as are plenty of butter and cream, especially in Normandy. Not surprisingly, for a country that is fiercely proud of its wine-making traditions, wine is used in cooking all over the country, but as this is usually the local wine, the same dish may display subtle variations from one place to another.

Bon appetit!

Regions

French food varies greatly from region to region, and great store is set by the use of traditional cooking methods and fresh local produce. Such cuisine has its roots back in the days when France's provinces were independent of each other, and each had its own unique culture and language.

NORMANDY

Normandy (Normandie) has an abundance of good things to eat, guaranteed to scupper the plans of even the strictest dieter. Its long coastline, which yields a rich harvest of seafood, is lined inland by lush green meadows dotted with grazing dairy cows, with cider-apple orchards and storybook timbered farmhouses.

Not surprisingly, Norman cuisine is inclined to be rich, being very much based on butter and cream. Mussels (*moules*), for instance, which are found in the bays of Mont St-Michel and Isigny, are served in a cream sauce here, rather than with the usual light version based on wine. This is also one of the few areas of France where you are likely to be served salted butter, unlike the rest of the country, where 'fresh' butter (unsalted) tends to be preferred.

If you are eating out, fresh oysters from St-Vaast-la-Hougue are a delicious starter. Staying with seafood, try the famous *sole normande* – a feast of seafood, including oysters and mussels served as a garnish for sole, which is coated in a cream sauce scented with truffles. If you are feeling more adventurous, sample other fish dishes such as *marmite dieppoise*, a mix of fish and shellfish cooked Dieppe-style, with leeks, cider and, of course, cream. Normandy also has its own version of *soupe de poisson* (fish soup). *Limande* is lemon sole and is used for cheaper dishes, *lisettes* are small mackerel, landed at the port of Dieppe, and *demoiselles de Cherbourg* are baby lobsters.

Many cities in this region have their own special dishes. Look out for the famous mouthwatering roast duck from Rouen (*canard rouennais*), specially bred locally. Stuffed with a mixture that includes its own liver, the duck is served with a red wine sauce. You can also find tripe, if you

Charming timber-framed houses at Beuvron-en-Auge, in Normandy.

A delicious speciality of Normandy, tarte normande.

are fond of this particular dish, served *à la mode de Caen* with root vegetables, leeks, cider, calves' feet and calvados. Tripe is also found in *andouillettes* (chitterling sausages) from Caen, Vire and Alençon.

Pork is often served Vallée d'Auge-style, flamed in Calvados, then cooked with apples and cream. This method is used for veal and chicken; turbot, another delicacy, is often cooked the same way. Pork turns up again in a variety of pâtés, sausages and some famous smoked chitterlings (pork offal) from Vire. Another Norman speciality is *boudin noir* (black pudding), especially *sanguette*, a highly prized version made from rabbit's blood, from the Orne. Lamb is mainly reared on the salt marsh (*pré-salé*) of the bay of Mont St-Michel.

Some of the great cheeses are from Normandy, notably the disc-shaped Camembert, with its creamy taste and distinctive white rind. The rectangular Pont-l'Evêque, with its yellow-orange exterior, comes from Normandy, too, where it is made near the picturesque fishing port of Honfleur. It smells more pungent than it tastes. If you do not already know it, try the equally strong-smelling Livarot, which is made in the cider country, the Pays d'Auge. Livarot has a harder texture, a spicy flavour and a rust-coloured crust.

Mouthwatering cakes and pastries to enjoy for dessert include *tarte normande* – a flan usually filled with apples, but you may find one made with pears. Then there are almond-flavoured custards to try, too, often laced with Calvados. Almonds are also used to make *mirlitons*, small light tarts from Rouen, while whole apples or pears sometimes appear cooked in pastry, known as *chaussons* or *rabottes*.

Normandy lacks only one thing: vineyards – its climate is too cold and too wet. But it makes up for that with cider and Calvados. The cider is quite unlike some mass-produced versions, being thirst-quenching and full of character, but do not underestimate its potency. Calvados is an apple brandy. For those who find it too strong, a pleasant alternative is Pommeau, a blend of Calvados and apple juice.

Bénédictine and other liqueurs are used in the luscious chocolates made in and around Fécamp.

THE NORTH AND CHAMPAGNE

With rivers abounding in fish and with one-third of all France's catch being landed at Boulogne-sur-Mer, it is not surprising that there is a huge selection of fish dishes to choose from here. First there is *bouillabaisse du nord*, a type of fish stew, then there is *matelote*, a freshwater-fish version to sample. Look out, too, for the delicious *cervelas de brochet*, sausages made from pike and potato. Eels (*anguilles*) are served jellied in wine, laced with herbs. There are also freshly caught trout (*truite*) to be had from the valleys of the Canche and Course.

Turkey is often served in this part of France. The best poultry comes from Licques. Chicken is often cooked in beer (*coq à la bière*) – evidence that Belgium is not far away – with juniper berries and, sometimes, a dash of gin added. Beer also appears in another favourite, *carbonnade de boeuf*, beef slow-cooked with onions and herbs.

Again, the best lamb is grazed on salt marshes, this time at the bay of the Somme. Look for the protected name '*Estran*'. Pork appears on the menu a great deal and pigs' trotters from Ste-Menehould are famous, served slow-cooked in white wine with herbs, then grilled. You may find sheep's trotters cooked this way, too.

Continuing to be more adventurous, *petits gris* snails, small and dark brown in colour, are a local delicacy, and some of the best frogs' legs (*cuisses de grenouilles*) in France come from the banks of the River

Somme. Wild duck from the same river is a traditional speciality that is becoming more scarce.

The soups cooked here are usually filling, with the most famous version being *potage St-Germain*, made from peas. *Potée champenoise*, another soup, does not, alas, contain champagne but only chicken, sausage and vegetables.

The *charcuterie* you will be served in restaurants, or that you may buy in the shops, tends to be on the hearty side. For instance, *andouilles* and *andouillettes* are much loved in this part of France, often eaten with cabbage and potatoes. From the Ardennes comes a delicious ham, smoked to a deep rosy-red colour. You may find rabbit on the menu, too, which is also made into a special black sausage, *boudin de lapin*. Pâté on sale may well be labelled *potjevfleische*, a Flemish name.

This area of France is known as a pastry cook's paradise. It is from here that gâteaux such as the famous St-Honoré originated. Sweets, for example, *bêtises de Cambrai*, a type of humbug, and sugared almonds, are also a speciality. You will also find some of the best bread in France here. If you like gingerbread, then you must try the local version, *pain d'épices*, while fans of spicy savouries should look out for *moutarde de Meaux*, a local granular mustard that goes very well with cold roast white meat.

Although there are some delicious local cheeses to try (Maroilles, for instance, with its pungent orange rind), Brie and the milder Coulommiers are the two best known.

It is here that the greatest wine of all is made, the world-famous champagne. When you have poured your glass of bubbly, you should accompany it with the elegant *biscuit de Reims*, a type of macaroon.

Beer is the northern drink, with hundreds of varieties and styles available, and micro-breweries thriving.

ALSACE–LORRAINE

This is pickled cabbage country: not only do the Alsatians eat *choucroute* (*sauerkraut*), but they produce it and can it, in vast quantities. As you approach Krautergersheim, near Obernai, where the cabbage fields are, if the wind is in the right direction, you may notice that there is an unmistakable whiff of cabbage in the air. Alsace has what is called a continental climate with hot sunny days in summer but chilly nights. Hearty food,

German-style, is the order of the day, with *choucroute garnie*, a dish of *sauerkraut* garnished with various types of sausages and pork, being the local dish. Just in case you feel there is not enough on the piled-high plate, they serve it with boiled potatoes too.

Other delicacies include *pâté de foie gras en croûte* (goose liver pâté wrapped in a pastry case) and goose liver pie seasoned with truffles. Goose is a staple on the menu, as are pheasants (*faisans*) and hares (*lièvres*). In addition, you will find essentially German sausages such as *cervelas* made from smoked pork; *mettwurst* made from beef; and *knack-wurst*, a frankfurter-style sausage. The most intriguing, however, is the *saucisse de Strasbourg*, the sausage from the culinary capital of the area. It is a mix of beef and pork, smoked and flavoured with caraway seeds. Also from Strasbourg comes *boeuf salé*, otherwise known as *pikefleisch* – depending on how near you are to the border – smoked brisket of beef.

Fish from the region's many clear rivers include trout (*truite*), pike (*brochet*) and crayfish (*écrevisse*), often served cooked in Riesling wine.

The Vosges mountains that divide Alsace from Lorraine act as a frontier of cuisine. Over on the Lorraine side the food becomes more French. This is the home, of course, of *quiche Lorraine*, the famous egg and bacon

The Alsace town of Riquewihr is surrounded by vineyards.

tart, and the *tarte Lorraine*, which is more filling and spicy, made with pork or veal and onions. There is also a *tarte flambée*, which could almost be described as a bacon, cream and onion pizza. The dishes of Lorraine tend to be lighter than those of Alsace, containing eggs, cheese and foods cooked in butter. Look out for *grillade à la Champagneules*, a kind of *croque-monsieur*, fried ham on toast, coated with a cheese and beer mix. And those with a sweet tooth should sample the jams, fruit tarts and pastries. Both Alsace and Lorraine specialise in fruits in syrup, such as plums, bilberries, cherries and raspberries, which are famous the world over. Plums of all varieties and redcurrants from Bar-le-Duc are also typical of the area.

Cheeses are not a particular speciality here but you should try the best one, Munster, made on the slopes of the Vosges. It is sometimes flavoured with cumin, caraway or anise seeds.

The region's wines, labelled by grape type, are mostly white and aromatic. Fruit *eaux-de-vie* (clear spirits) and a huge amount of beer are also produced.

BRITTANY

The craggy coastline of Brittany (Bretagne) edges a land of contrasts where, not far from the wild and windy peninsula of Finistère, is the market garden of France. Its mild climate, thanks to the Gulf Stream, enables the Bretons to grow early spring vegetables and, from late spring on, delicious strawberries from Plougastel. Melons, dessert grapes, walnuts and pears are all foods to enjoy in this part of France, which varies in climate from the rainy north to the sunny beaches of places such as La Baule.

Some of the best shellfish in the world comes from here; for instance, delicate Belon oysters from the Pont-Aven area, lobster (*homard*) and clams (*palourdes*). This is the home of *homard à l'armoricaine*, lobster cooked in oil with onions or shallots, tomatoes, white wine and brandy. *Coquilles St-Jacques* (scallops) also hail from here, and the local equivalent of *bouillabaisse*, the famous Provençal fish stew, is *cotriade*, which is white fish cooked with mussels, onions, potatoes, herbs and cream. If you have time, try to visit one of the picturesque fish markets such as those at St-Malo, Quiberon or Loctudy, to watch the excitement of the day's catch arriving. Breton chickens are good, too, renowned for their succulence and

Brittany is famous for the quality of its shellfish.

plumpness, and pork is used for some excellent *pâté de campagne* and other items of charcuterie.

Of course, this is pancake country, and you can eat an entire, very cheap meal in a *crêperie*. Start with a seafood *crêpe*, move on to your choice of savoury *galette*, a heavier pancake made with buckwheat flour, then finish with one drenched in kirsch for dessert.

Cheeses here are inclined to be mild, with St-Paulin, with its bright orange rind, being best known. Butter is usually salted. Increasingly popular are varieties with whole salt crystals dotted throughout. *Beurre de baratte* is made with mature cream for a richer flavour. Brittany boasts many traditional cakes, but the best-known version is called *quatre-quarts* (four quarters), a light but firm sponge. It is often mixed with candied fruit, almonds and raisins.

No wine is made in Brittany, but if you want a bottle to go with your seafood, choose something from the Loire, just beyond Brittany's borders. A Muscadet *sur lie* would do nicely.

Finally, do not go home without a traditional plait of the famous red-skinned Breton onions, which are grown near Roscoff.

A metal bridge crosses the Loire to the town of St-Mathurin-sur-Loire in the distance.

THE LOIRE VALLEY

The long, lazy Loire meanders its way to the sea through a mild countryside of castles and caves – some of the best wine cellars in France – ending in the majestic port of Nantes. There are some 200,000 hectares/500,000 acres of vineyards here, producing wines as diverse as the fruity reds of Touraine, and Vouvray, a sparkling alternative to champagne. As you would expect from an area that produces great wines, the food from the Loire valley is elegant.

As the area is laced with streams and tributaries, freshwater fish abound; pike (*brochet*), carp (*carpe*), salmon (*saumon*) and eel (*anguille*) are plentiful. Chicken, rabbit and pork appear, too, and the *Châteaubriand* steak is thought by many to be named after a small town here. You will find *haricot de mouton* served, too, which, strictly speaking, should not have haricot beans in it at all, for it comes from an old word *halicot*, meaning to chop. Look out, too, for appetising *rillettes* made from shredded pork meat – delicious spread on thick slices of country bread – as well as hare and partridge terrines. Game from the marshy Sologne is renowned.

This is a major mushroom-producing area, the region's limestone caves being ideal for the cultivation of tiny white *champignons*. So it is not surprising that they appear in many local dishes. And if you are there in the spring, eat locally grown asparagus, especially the Vineuil-St-Claude variety, which grows in the fine sands bordering the River Loire, not far from the famous Château de Chambord.

Vegetables appear prominently on the menu and in the markets – be sure to look out for pumpkins, potatoes and cabbage, in particular. *Truffiat* is the name of a potato cake, and *bardatte* refers to a dish of cabbage stuffed with hare.

For dessert you will probably buy or be offered the speciality of the area, *gâteau de Pithiviers*, a puff pastry tart filled with almond paste. Another favourite French dessert hails from the region. *Tarte tatin*, named after the Tatin sisters at whose restaurant it was created, is a stickily delicious upside-down tart of apples and caramel.

Local cheeses to look out for include the pyramid-shaped Valençay, a goats' milk cheese with a coating of ash, and Feuille de Dreux, a cheese made from cows' milk, shaped like a Camembert and covered with chestnut leaves.

The wines of the Loire are legion; among the whites try Sauvignon, Sancerre and Vouvray. To go with shellfish, there is the famous Muscadet (see pages 94–5 for more on the wines of the Loire valley). But perhaps one of the best-known drinks from this area is Cointreau, the orange-flavoured liqueur.

BURGUNDY AND FRANCHE-COMTÉ

Beautiful Burgundy (Bourgogne), basking in the sun, is as renowned for its food as for its wines, which include Beaujolais, as well as the world-famous Côtes de Beaune and Chablis.

Sample some of the good living here, for both game and fish abound in great quantity, and the white Charolais cattle, which are known throughout the world, produce superb meat. The ubiquitous pig, too, provides the usual selection of *charcuterie* and dishes to be found elsewhere in France. A speciality here is *jambon persillé* – pressed ham layered with parsley and aspic – served cold. A strangely named sausage you will find in Franche-Comté is Jésus de Morteau, which tastes very akin to salami.

When it comes to dining out, start your meal with a *matelote*, fresh-water fish made into a soup with red wine, or *oeufs en meurette*, eggs poached in a red wine sauce. Or, if you like snails, try them *à la bourguignonne*, served hot and stuffed with garlic-flavoured butter with parsley.

The dish that is probably most famous in this area is *coq au vin*, chicken flamed in brandy then poached in good red wine with tiny whole onions and button mushrooms. Another delicious speciality is *boeuf bourguignon*, beef slow-cooked in a sauce made with young red wine. *Lapin à la moutarde* (rabbit in a mustard sauce) appears on the menu, too, using the famous mustard from Dijon (remember to take a pot home) – see recipe, pages 144–5.

The rivers, lakes and streams of Burgundy and Franche-Comté are full of fish, so *quenelles de brochet* (dumplings made from pike) often appear on the menu, as does *pochouse*, a stew made from a mix of fish in white wine – it becomes *meurette* when the wine used is red. Another classic Burgundian savoury of a lighter kind is *gougère*, a ring or small bun of choux pastry flavoured with Gruyère cheese.

Burgundy's best cheeses are those whose rinds are washed in *marc*, a spirit made from grape must. Epoisses is the most common example. From Franche-Comté come Gruyère-like Comté and the winter speciality Vacherin-Mont-d'Or, which can be spooned straight from its box.

The orchards and fruit fields of Burgundy are the inspiration behind the many wonderful fruit tarts you will find in the *pâtisseries*, including a tart made from bilberries (*myrtilles*). The fruit flavours are preserved too in *eau-de-vie*, white brandy with plums, raspberries or bilberries. *Crème de cassis*, the famous liqueur, is made from blackcurrants grown on the Burgundy hillsides. Mix it with white wine to make a refreshing aperitif called *kir*. Candied fruits and jams are popular also, particularly the delicious fruit-packed *confitures*, conserves made in Bar-le-Duc and Gevrey-Chambertin.

If the opportunity to sample French home-baking arises, you may be offered *nonnettes de Dijon* (iced gingerbread cake) and the *madeleines* of Commercy (little sponge cakes).

Where do you begin with the wines of Burgundy? White wine names such as Chablis and Montrachet spring to mind, while for red wine drinkers there are the great red burgundies from the Côte d'Or and simpler reds from the Beaujolais district. The wines of the Jura, in Franche-Comté, include two unusual varieties. *Vin jaune* resembles a Fino sherry, while the rare *vin de paille* is a superb sweet wine made from grapes dried on beds of straw (*paille*). See pages 93–4 for more on the wines of Burgundy.

The lake at La Clayette, in Burgundy, at dusk.

BORDEAUX AND THE SOUTHEAST

This is the land of the goose, and of good living. It shares with Normandy a tendency to use butter and cream in its cuisine, rather than oil, but many dishes are also cooked in goose fat.

This is a place to feast on truffles and *foie gras*; these two ingredients are almost always included in any dish marked *périgourdine*. The truffles come from the region's forests, where they are sought out by specially trained dogs or pigs, and fetch amazing prices at the market. If you are there in winter, when they are in season, and decide to buy one, treat it like black gold, for that is what it is known as locally. To make your truffle go a long way – for it is unlikely you will want to buy more than one – place it in a bowl of eggs. Its delicate flavour will permeate their shells and you will have a clutch of truffle-flavoured eggs for omelettes. In local restaurants you will probably find truffles featured in the famous local dish *brouillade périgourdine*, where they are cooked with scrambled eggs. You will also find plenty of wild mushrooms on sale in the markets.

Although goose holds pride of place on the menu, it is mainly eaten in the form of *pâté de foie gras* (goose liver pâté). The bird is seldom served roasted but is braised with wine and vegetables, served stuffed with plums (*oie farcie aux pruneaux*), or cooked and stored in its own fat in stoneware jars (*confit d'oie*).

You will find ducks on sale, too, and turkeys, which are becoming more and more common in the Dordogne. Pork is also popular and you may be served suckling pig. There are splendid locally cured hams available from Poitou. From the bountiful countryside and forests come all sorts of gamey delights such as guinea fowl (*pintadeau*), hare (*lièvre*), which is served jugged (*civet de lièvre*), and plenty of woodpigeons (*palombes*). Beef is good here, too, and an *entrecôte à la bordelaise* comes with a classic sauce made of red wine, shallots and the essential touch of tarragon. The famous *pré-salé* lamb of Pauillac, from sheep grazed on the banks of the Gironde, is also delicious, served, almost inevitably, with truffles. *Charcuterie* includes the full-flavoured *saucisse de Toulouse*, which features in that city's version of *cassoulet*, the hearty bean and meat stew of the south (see recipe, pages 139–40). This is also snail country; look out for them served Languedoc-style, with nuts, anchovies and tomatoes.

Good freshwater fish such as shad (*alose*) and barbel (*barbeau*) is widely available. A favourite dish in this part of the world is a *friture*, a fry-up of freshwater fish. Another very filling dish from the Poitou is a *chaudrée*, which is a stew of conger eel and white fish cooked together with potatoes, garlic and white wine. It was originally cooked in a cauldron (*chaudron*) – hence the name.

There are oysters from La Rochelle and, as a curiosity, you could try lamprey (*lamproie*), the eel-like creature that comes from the estuary of the River Gironde. It has a poisonous thread that must be taken out before cooking, therefore making it safer to eat it in a restaurant, where it is often served with root vegetables and a wine sauce. The Atlantic coastline is the source of some of France's best oysters, which are well worth trying when you are staying near the coast.

The lush green countryside of this region yields plenty of succulent young spring vegetables. Later come green beans and super-large Marmande tomatoes, a speciality of the area, which are excellent served stuffed. Above all, this is the place to try delicious young broad beans (*fèves*). In late summer, shallots are plentiful, too, and in autumn the pumpkins (*potirons*) arrive.

At the same time the fruits in season include greengages (*reines-Claude*) and yellow plums (*prunes*). Chestnuts and walnuts abound here, and are used to produce both sweet and savoury dishes. This is one of the few places in Europe where you can buy chestnut flour (*pain de paysans*).

The cheeses of this region are usually made from goats' milk (*chèvre*), such as the deliciously creamy Caillebotes and the Cabécou, which are traditionally served wrapped in chestnut leaves. Rocamadour cheese, on the other hand, can also be made from ewes' milk, depending on the season when it is made.

On the dessert front, look out for pancakes made with maize flour called, variously, *tourteaux* and *cruchades*. Almond-based biscuits are a speciality of this area, as is *fougasse*, which is a rich cake-type bread.

With the vineyards of Bordeaux on the doorstep, some of the best wines in France, the clarets – the Médocs, St-Émilions and so on – are there for the buying. But try, too, the local wines of the Dordogne and its neighbouring regions, the deep dark red Cahors, for instance. Cognac is the great brandy from Charente but if you are staying in the area, try the innumerable local nut liqueurs, too – *eau de noix* and the sweeter *crème de noix*, made from walnuts – and Ratafia, made from various plants or fruit. These are drinks you will find nowhere else.

The lush green hills of the Parc Régional des Volcans d'Auvergne.

AUVERGNE

The lush green pastures and mild climate of Auvergne are ideal for cattle-raising. Though winters can be cold, in the summer the cows roam on the mountain pastures watched over by herdsmen who live in *burons*, huts far from their home villages. This is where, in the past, they made the famous Cantal cheeses.

Charcuterie is excellent here, for the pigs of Auvergne provide excellent pork. Every town has its own local speciality, and it is worthwhile seeking it out; St-Flour, for instance, produces a delicacy called *friand sanflorain*, made of pork meat with herbs in a pastry case. There are pâtés as well, made as smooth as silk or rough-cut, country-style. There is black pudding with chestnuts (*boudin aux châtaignes*), peppered ham (*jambon au poivre*) and raw mountain hams (*jambons crus*).

Food tends to be on the hearty side, starting with *soupe aux choux*, made from cabbage, usually with ham or pork. Dishes that are typical of this part of the world include *tripoux*, delicious mutton feet and veal tripe stuffed and seasoned with herbs and cloves; then there is *potée auvergnate*, a typical country stew containing a rich blend of vegetables, salt pork and sausages. Another great favourite is *truffado*, a cheese and potato pancake spiked with garlic, while *pommes de terre au lard* is a tasty mix of potato, bacon and onions with herbs. *Aligot* is another delicious potato dish made with puréed potatoes and Cantal cheese. Lentils from Le Puy appear in many dishes.

The region's most famous dessert features the black *guignes* cherries grown here. In *clafoutis* they are baked in a sweet, egg-rich batter. Other varieties, and indeed other fruit, may also be used.

The cheeses of the Auvergne are legendary. As well as the classic Cantal, a semi-firm yellow cheese with a nutty flavour, St-Nectaire, which comes in flat discs, has an elusive flavour of hazelnuts. Also nutty-flavoured are such local goats' milk cheeses as Galette de la Chaise Dieu and Brique du Forez. The *bleus d'Auvergne*, the creamy blue- and sometimes green-veined cheeses, have a flavour that is fresh and slightly sharp, while Fourme d'Ambert is a veined cheese that was being made, it is claimed, even before Julius Caesar invaded Gaul. There are dozens of small cheese-makers still operating in the Auvergne, most of them on mountain farms, and it pays to keep a look-out for them when driving through the countryside.

It is worthwhile trying the local wines here – the Côtes d'Auvergne, which is produced near Clermont-Ferrand, or the light reds of Châteaugay, for instance. If you would prefer a bracing cordial, pick Verveine du Velay, which contains 32 plants, including wild verbena. There are two types: the yellow, which is sweet and subtle, or the green, which has a stronger flavour. However, perhaps the most famous drink of this volcanic region is water, with household names such as Vichy and Volvic hailing from here.

PROVENCE

The very name Provence conjures up a picture of a sun-soaked countryside, filled with olive trees, sunflowers and herbs. Once you cross the line where the roofs of the houses change to those distinctive terracotta tiles, and the temperature soars, olive oil becomes the staple ingredient in which food is cooked. It is said that the Italians first taught the French to cook, and the nearer you get to the Italian border, the more often pasta appears on the menu.

The Mediterranean inevitably exerts its influence, and Marseille is the home of some splendid fish soups, notably the traditional *bouillabaisse*. This, it must be said, is more than just a soup. It is a whole meal, in which your plate is heaped high with a mix of seafish seasoned strongly with garlic and herbs, coloured by saffron, with a slice of bread on the top. The actual soup – the broth in which the fish was cooked – is usually served as the first course. Any number of fish may be used to make *bouillabaisse*, but it must contain *rascasse* (scorpion fish), which looks like a miniature red mullet. Those who feel that the *bouillabaisse* experience is too much for them should ask for *soupe de poisson* instead – when the fish is puréed, the taste is less obviously fishy. To go with these soups, and many other dishes, comes *rouille*, a spicy mayonnaise-like sauce flavoured with chillies, garlic and saffron.

Basil is the south's favourite herb, and you will find it features in another Provençal favourite, *soupe au pistou*, cooked with a mix of vegetables and basil paste like the Italian *pesto*.

Olives and anchovies are the staple ingredients of a number of Provençal dishes, the famous *salade niçoise*, for instance, in which they are mixed with green beans, tomatoes, sometimes tuna and hard-boiled eggs. Aubergines (eggplants), peppers, courgettes and tomatoes are combined in the delicious *ratatouille*. *Aïoli* is a garlic mayonnaise, but a *grand aïoli* is a whole meal centred around it, with vegetables, meat, eggs and snails to dip into the sauce.

The Italian influence makes itself felt with items such as *pissaladière*, a speciality of Nice, which is in fact a version of the pizza, usually made as a square rather than a round tart.

CORSICA

The food of Corsica (Corse) is, in the main, similar to that of the South of France. It does tend, however, to be slightly spicier and more robust – as are the Corsican wines, particularly the rather heavy reds.

Look out for wild boar pâtés, home-cured hams – in fact, all kinds of *charcuterie*. The sheep's and goats' milk cheeses here are good. Brocciu is usually served as a fresh, Ricotta-like cheese, though it is sometimes allowed to harden and mature. Seafood on offer includes bass (*bar* or *loup*), sardines and squid (*calamar*), but look out for unusual items as well, such as sea urchins (*oursins*). Chestnuts are widely used – with cereal production difficult, the island's bread is traditionally made using chestnut flour.

Relaxed outdoor dining in Nice, on France's famous Côte d'Azur.

A–Z of French Food

A

Abats

The generic French name for offal, liver, feet, heart and so on. The French eschew waste and tend to eat parts of the animal others might throw away. So it is not surprising to find heads, lungs, stomach, feet, even testicles (*animelles*) served. The names for those parts you are most likely to come across, in case you wish to avoid them, are also in this section.

Agneau

Lamb. *Agneau de lait* is milk-fed, ie baby lamb, while *agneau pascal* is spring lamb.

Agneau de pré-salé

This phrase is found in menus all over France, but notably in Picardy, Brittany, Normandy, Bordeaux and the Vendée. It describes meat from lambs that have grazed on salty meadows (*pré-salé*) washed by the sea. The meat is always served young and usually roasted, sometimes, but not always, without strong seasonings such as garlic or onion. It is not salty, but sweet and aromatic, and is highly prized.

Aiglefin, aigrefin

Haddock.

Aïgo Boulido

A Provençal garlic soup, similar to that found in Spain and Portugal. Traditionally served poured over slices of bread. It may also be served with an egg in it, and topped with *croûtons* or fried bread.

Aïgo saou

Garlic soup made with fish and potatoes.

Aiguille

Also known as *orphie*. Needlefish or garfish. One of the many delicious Mediterranean fish that you find on French menus. Do not be put off by the colour of the bones – they are mauve when cooked (although they are green in the raw fish).

Ail

Garlic. Garlic is used liberally in French cooking.

Aillade

A sauce made from garlic and oil, found throughout the country in slightly varying forms. Often served with snails.

Aïoli

The classic garlic mayonnaise from Provence. You will find it served with *crudités* (raw vegetables) as a starter and also with a special dish that is something of an acquired taste, *brandade de morue*.

Aïoli garni

A special stew of salted cod (*morue*) from Provence. It also includes vegetables, maybe meat, and a garnish of snails.

Airelles

Cranberries, whortleberries or bilberries.

Allache

Large sardine.

Allumette

Match: but it is also used to describe very thin-cut potato chips. The same word is sometimes used for small sticks of puff pastry.

Alose

Shad. Bony fish like a large herring.

Alouette

Lark. Under EC rules, the French are not allowed to kill small birds such as larks for food, but you will occasionally find canned lark pâté on sale.

Alouette sans tête

Thin slices of veal or beef, rolled round a savoury filling.

Aloyau

Beef sirloin.

Alsacienne, à l'

Food cooked Alsace-style inevitably comes with *choucroute* (pickled cabbage), ham and frankfurter-style sausages.

Amuse-gueules

Literally 'amuse-mouth': tiny appetisers, usually miniature savoury pastries – quiches, for instance – served with *apéritifs* in many restaurants.

Ananas

Pineapple.

Anchoïade

A pungent Provençal paste of anchovies and garlic. It is used as a spread on toast as an appetiser in southern meals, or served sometimes with *crudités* as an *hors d'oeuvre*.

Andouilles

Cooked pork sausage with strips of chitterling inside it. Served cold as a first course in restaurant meals. *Andouilles* are on sale everywhere. They can be rather chewy and not to everyone's liking.

Andouillettes

Small chitterling sausages. Usually served hot with mustard.

Aneth

Dill.

Ange de mer or angelot

Angelfish. This is a member of the shark family but in culinary terms it resembles skate, since it has wing-shaped fins.

Anglaise, à l'

'In the English way'. Meaning boiled, or with boiled vegetables, which shows what the French think of English cooking. The same phrase is used to describe any dish that is typically British.

Anguille

Freshwater eel.

Anguillettes
Very small eels served in the Basque country. The French are very fond of eels, which they eat both hot and cold, and garnished with quite elaborate sauces.

Animelles
Testicles. Usually served fried, they taste better than they look, but are not everyone's ideal dish.

Annot
A Provençal cheese made from ewes' or goats' milk.

Appellation d'Origine Contrôlée (AOC)
A form of quality control primarily reserved for wine but it may also be awarded to foods – Puy lentils or Bresse poultry and specific cheeses, for instance. More information on the AOC system is given in Wine Facts, pages 102–05.

Arachide
Peanut.

Araignée de mer
Spider crab.

Arapède
Limpet.

Ardennaise, à l'
Meat cooked Ardennes-style, usually with juniper berries.

Arlésienne, à l'
Fish or meat cooked Arles-style with tomatoes, onions and olives.

Armoricaine, à l'
Usually fish, especially lobster, cooked Breton-style with brandy, white wine, herbs, tomatoes and onions.

Armotte
Like Italian *polenta*, maize flour cooked in goose fat. From Gascony, it is eaten instead of bread and rice.

Arômes de Lyon
A cheese with a strong taste, soaked in white wine, often wrapped in vine leaves.

Artichaut
Globe artichoke.

Asperge
Asparagus. *Pointe d'asperge* is asparagus tip. Asparagus is normally served with a butter or hollandaise sauce.

Assiette
Dish, plate.

Assiette anglaise
A mixture of cold meats.

Assiette de fruits de mer
A plate of seafood.

Aurin
Grey mullet (in the South of France).

Auvergne, Bleu d'
Salty blue cheese from Auvergne with a creamy texture. Made from cows' milk, it is sold in circular packs all over France.

Avocat
Avocado.

B

Baba au rhum
A yeasted 'cake' soaked with

Globe artichokes are a favourite and colourful purchase at France's many markets.

rum-flavoured syrup. Found in most parts of France. If you buy one from a *pâtisserie*, be prepared to eat it with a spoon.

Badasco
Provençal name for *rascasse* (fish). Used in *bouillabaisse* and fish soup, but not usually served on its own.

Baeckeoffe
Layered meat casserole with potatoes, onions and white wine, from Alsace.

Baguette
Long stick-shaped loaf of bread.

Baie de ronce
Blackberry.

Baie
Berry.

Baiser
Confection of meringues sandwiched together with cream.

Bajoue
Pig's cheek.

Ballotine
Meat pie or *galantine*. Eaten cold.

Banane
Banana. Served sometimes with cream and kirsch (*bananes baronnet*) or with rum, sugar and macaroons (*bananes Beauharnis*).

Banon
Small cream cheese from Provence made from ewes', goats' or cows' milk and sold as flat discs or in cylinders. It is wrapped in chestnut leaves or placed on balsa wood.

Bar
Sea bass. There are more than 60 different names for sea bass in French, notably *badèche, cernier, bézuque* and *loup de mer*.

Barbadine
Passion fruit.

Barbe-à-papa
Candyfloss – literally, 'father's beard'.

Barbeau
Barbel, an unexciting, bony fresh-water fish that may be casseroled with wine, typically in the Loire valley and Burgundy.

Barberey
Soft cheese from the Champagne region, cured in ashes.

Barberon
The name for salsify in the South of France. This long, thin root vegetable may be served with butter or coated in white sauce.

Barbue
Brill, a flat fish, sometimes served baked in tomato sauce with vegetables (*brancas*); or fried in oil with tomato, aubergine (eggplant) and garlic sauce (*à la toulonnaise*).

Barquette
Boat-shaped pastry, rather like a small tart or flan.

Basilic
Basil.

Basquaise, à la
Food cooked Basque-style, with tomatoes, peppers and rice.

Batavia
A type of bitter lettuce (see also *scarole*).

Baton
Small stick of bread.

Baudroie
Monkfish.

Bavarois
A cream and custard dessert, usually with fruit.

You'll be able to find some exotic fruit, such as passion fruit, at street markets in France.

Bavette
Skirt of beef.

Baveuse
Runny – an omelette may be served *baveuse*, with a still-liquid centre.

Béarnaise
Classic sauce made mayonnaise-style, flavoured with tarragon. Often served with steak.

Beaufort, Beaufort de Montagne
A firm Gruyère-type cows' milk cheese with few or, more often, no holes in it. From Haute-Savoie.

Bécasse or bécasseau
Woodcock. Served roasted with truffles (*à la Diane*) or on fried bread with *foie gras* (*à la riche*).

Bécassine
Snipe.

Béchamel
White sauce, flavoured with bay or a hint of onion.

Bedeu
Provençal name for tripe.

Beignet
Fritter – sweet or savoury.

Belle-Hélène
Ice-cream and chocolate sauce as served with pear.

Belon
Breton oyster.

Belval
A firm mild cheese with a shiny rind, from Picardy.

Berawecka, Bireweck
Spicy bread roll from Alsace with dried fruit and kirsch.

Bercy
With a wine, shallot and bone marrow sauce (usually served with steak).

Bergère, à la
Chicken or meat cooked 'the shepherdess's way', with ham, mushrooms, onions and match-stick potatoes.

Bethmale
A hard spicy cylindrical cheese from Touraine, made from cows' milk.

Betterave
Beetroot. Sometimes served Provençal-style with anchovies and hard-boiled eggs.

Beurre
Butter. Usually sold and served unsalted in France, the exceptions being Normandy and Brittany. *Beurre demi-sel* is slightly salted.

Beurre blanc
Sauce from the Loire made with butter, white wine and shallots.

Beurre de Provence
Not butter at all, but a local name for *aïoli*.

Beurre maître d'hôtel
Butter blended with lemon juice and parsley. Used to top a slice of fish or meat.

Beurre marchand de vin
Butter with red wine, meat juices and shallots.

Beurre meunière, noisette
Browned butter with lemon juice and parsley.

Beurre noir
Blackened butter. Often served with skate.

Biche
Doe, venison. See *chevreuil*.

Bifteck
Steak. *Bien cuit* is well-done, *à point* is medium, while *bleu* or *saignant* is underdone, ie rare. *Bifteck haché* is French for hamburger, but nowadays you are likely to see it called simply a hamburger.

Bifteck tartare
Chopped beef served raw with tartare sauce or raw egg and onion.

Bigorneau, biou
Winkle.

Bis
Meaning brown, wholemeal, usually used in connection with flour or bread.

Biscotin
Sweet biscuit.

Biscotte
Rusk.

Biscuit
Sponge cake. A *biscuit à la cuiller* is a sponge finger, a *biscuit sec* is a plain biscuit.

Bisque
Thick creamy soup, usually of shellfish, made with white wine, cream and tomatoes. If it is described as *bisque aux légumes*, it is a thick vegetable soup made with lentils.

Blanc d'oeuf
White of egg.

Blanchaille
Whitebait.

Blanquette
White meat cooked in a white sauce.

Blé
Corn, wheat.

Blé noir
Buckwheat. Used for some pancakes (*galettes*) in Brittany.

Blette
Swiss chard.

Bleu
Blue. The rarest steak, even rarer than *saignant* ('bleeding'). Also a way of poaching trout that gives the skin a blueish hue.

Boeuf
Beef.

Boeuf bourguignon(ne), à la
The classic French dish of beef casseroled in red burgundy wine with onions and mushrooms (see recipe, page 142).

Boeuf en daube
Beef braised with wine, onions, carrots and herbs.

Boeuf estouffade
A type of *daube*, or stew, cooked with pigs' trotters.

Bombe glacée
Moulded ice-cream dessert, usually one flavour filled with another, for example, *bombe cardinal* (vanilla and raspberry ice-cream).

Bonbel
Brand name of a small mild hard cheese from St-Paulin, found on sale in most supermarkets.

Bondon
A sweet.

Bonite
Bonito. A fish similar to tuna, but smaller.

Bonne femme
Poached in white wine with mushrooms, eg *sole bonne femme*.

Bordelaise, à la
Cooked Bordeaux-style, usually in a red wine sauce with shallots, tarragon and bone marrow.

Bossons macérés
A goats' milk cheese you may find locally in the Languedoc, soaked in oil, white wine and *marc* (brandy). It is rather strong and something of an acquired taste.

Bouchée
A mouthful, for example, *bouchée à la reine*, a small savoury vol-au-vent.

Boudin blanc
A white pudding, a type of sausage, usually pork or poultry. Sold studded with truffles at New Year. It is served poached in a sauce or in wine.

Boudin noir
Black (blood) pudding.

Bouillabaisse
Hearty Mediterranean fish stew from Marseille. The liquid is often served as a soup, the fish as a main course. There are various versions of this; *bouillinade*, for instance, is a fish stew from Roussillon with onions, garlic, peppers and potatoes.

Bouillon
Stock or broth.

Boulangère, à la
Oven-baked, often, in the case of meat, with potatoes.

Boule de neige
Sponge or ice-cream dessert covered with whipped cream.

Bouquet
A name for a prawn.

Bourdaine
Apple dumpling with jam. Served as a sweet in Anjou.

Bourgeoise, à la
Braised meat or chicken with bacon, carrots and onions.

Bourguignon(ne), à la
Cooked Burgundy-style. See *boeuf à la bourguignon(ne)*.

Bourride
A white fish stew from the South of France. Served with *aïoli* or *rouille*.

Boursotto
A pastry filled with vegetables, rice, anchovies and cheese, from Nice.

Boutargue
Dried, salted and pressed roe, usually grey mullet, from Provence. Served thinly sliced with olive oil and lemon juice.

Bouteille
Bottle.

Branche, en
Whole, as in vegetables – eg, broccoli, spinach.

Brandade de morue
Paste from the Languedoc made from salted cod, soaked until soft, cooked, pounded with olive oil and milk or cream. Garlic may be added. Served with fresh or toasted bread. The *brandade* may be browned in the oven before serving. Very much an acquired taste.

Brandade de thon
Canned tuna mixed with haricot beans, from Brittany.

Brème
Bream.

Brème de mer
Sea bream.

Bresaola
Sliced, dried salted beef from the South of France.

Bressan
A mild goats' milk farmhouse cheese from Bresse.

Bresse, Bleu de
Cows' milk blue cheese with a creamy consistency, made in and around the town of Bresse.

Bresse, poulet de
Considered by many to be France's finest chicken.

Bretonne, à la
Cooked Breton-style, in onion sauce with haricot beans.

Bretonneau
Turbot.

Brie
Soft cheese with a creamy, sometimes runny, centre from the Île-de-France. Brie de Coulommiers is factory-made, while Brie de Meaux is farm-made.

Brillat-Savarin
A mild classic French cheese from Normandy with a triple cream content and a buttery texture.

Brioche
A sweet breakfast roll made from yeasted dough, with eggs and butter.

Broche, à la
Spit-roasted.

Brochet
Pike. Often served in the form of *quenelles* (fish dumplings).

Brochet de mer
Barracuda, a fine-flavoured white fish with very large, firm flakes. Good cold with mayonnaise, or served hot.

Brochette
Skewer.

Broufado
A traditional beef stew with vinegar, anchovies and capers, from Provence.

Brouillé
Scrambled. *Oeufs brouillés* or *brouillade* is scrambled eggs.

Brûlé
Flamed.

Brut
Raw, or dry.

Visitors to France can expect to find a mouth-watering array of bread and pastries.

Bûche

Literally, 'log'. A rolled-up or log-shaped cake, such as *bûche de Noël*, a chocolate Christmas cake.

Bugne

A sweet fritter from Lyon.

C

Cabassol/les

Lamb offal (eg, the head, trotters, tripe) cooked with vegetables and ham. This is a local dish from the Languedoc.

Cabécou

Round soft cheese from Périgord, made with goats' or ewes' milk.

Cabillaud or cabeliau

Fresh cod. See also *morue*.

Cabot

Chub, a bony freshwater fish.

Cacahuète

Peanut.

Cacao

Cocoa.

Cachat

Round, rindless Provençal cheese made from ewes' milk, with a strong flavour. It is often aged in vinegar.

Cachir

Kosher.

Caille or cailleteau

Quail. Cooked variously with truffles (*à la gourmande*), wrapped in vine leaves (*à la dauphinoise*) or with white grapes (*aux raisins*).

Cake

If you see this word on the menu, it means British-style fruit cake.

Calamar or calmar

Squid.

Camard
Gurnard, a seafish that is similar to mullet.

Camarguaise, à la
Cooked the Camargue way, with tomatoes, garlic, herbs, orange peel, olives and wine or brandy.

Camembert
Famous round cheese with soft centre from Normandy but which is available everywhere.

Canard, caneton or canardeau
Duck. *Confit de canard* is duck preserved in its own fat.

Canard, maigret/magret de
Duck breast, usually cooked rare and served thinly sliced. Also sold smoked in thin slivers for use in salads. The breast should be taken from a duck that was fattened for its liver.

Canard(s), salmi(s) de
Roasted duck, served in a white wine sauce.

Canard sauvage
Wild duck.

Cancoillotte
A type of cheese spread made from heated whey. Sometimes served on *croûtons* of toasted bread, a dish from Jura.

Caneton rouennais
Roast, pressed duckling.

Canneberge
Cranberry.

Cannelle
Cinnamon

Cantal or Cantalet
Nutty, firm cylindrical cheese from the *Département* of Cantal in Auvergne. Made from cows' milk, it is quite widely available.

Many local French cheeses, such as Pont l'Évêque and Camembert, will be familiar.

Caprice des Dieux
Brand name of creamy oval cheese from Champagne.

Carbonnade
Braised, sometimes fried or grilled, meat.

Carbonnade de boeuf à la flamande
A famous dish of beef and onions cooked in beer, from the north of France.

Cardeau
Sardine.

Cargolade
Snails cooked in wine, or barbecued, from Languedoc-Roussillon.

Cari
Curry powder.

Carotte
Carrot.

Carottes vichy
Carrots glazed with sugar and butter.

Carpe or carpeau
Carp. Bony freshwater fish with a subtle, and to some people unexciting, taste.

Carpion
A type of trout.

Carré de Bray
Soft, slightly salty, square cheese from Normandy.

Carrelet
Plaice.

Casse-croûte
Snack.

Casserole, en
Cooked in a saucepan, not in a casserole.

Casseron
Cuttlefish.

Cassis
Blackcurrant.

Cassolette
Little dish of food, usually an appetiser or dessert.

Cassoulet
Pork, mutton or lamb, sometimes goose, with bacon and sausage cooked with haricot beans in an earthenware dish, from the Languedoc (see recipe, page 139).

Cata
Dogfish.

Caudière, Caudrée
Fish and potato chowder from northern France.

Causalade, oeufs à la
Fried eggs and bacon.

Caviar niçois
Anchovy, olive and herb paste pounded in olive oil.

Cédrat
Large, sour citrus fruit.

Celan
Sardine.

Céleri-rave
Celeriac. *Céleri rémoulade* is grated celeriac in mayonnaise.

Cendré d'Aisy
Strong-smelling cheese from Burgundy, cured in ashes and *marc* (brandy).

Cèpe
Wild mushroom; *bolet* (*boletus*).
A large variety of fungi are eaten
in France, many of them looking
quite unlike mushrooms. You will
find them on sale, fresh or dried,
in greengrocers' shops and in
the market. They have a more
pungent smell and taste stronger
than ordinary mushrooms and are
slightly chewy.

Cèpes à la mode bordelaise
Mushrooms cooked in oil with
shallots, garlic and parsley.

Cerise
Cherry.

Cerises jubilé
Cherries served hot, flamed
with kirsch.

Cervelas
Lightly smoked pork sausage
with garlic.

Cervelas de poisson
Fish loaf made with pike, from
Champagne.

Cervelles
Brains, usually calf.

Chabichou
Sweet-tasting, very small goats'
milk cheese from Poitou.

Champignon
Cultivated mushroom.
Champignons de Paris are
button mushrooms.

Chanterelle
Wild mushroom with a distinct
yellow tinge.

Chantilly, crème
Sweet whipped cream.

Charbon de bois, au
Charcoal-grilled.

Charcuterie
The collective term for prepared
and/or cooked pork products, and
the shop that sells them.

Charlotte
Hot pudding of apples baked with
buttered bread.

Charlotte Russe
Cold cream custard set in a mould
lined with sponge fingers.

Chasseur
Cooked in the hunter's way with
wine, mushrooms and shallots.

Châtaigne
Chestnut.

Châteaubriand
Thick steak, usually serving
two people.

Chaud, chaude
Hot.

Chaudeu
Orange-flavoured tart from Nice.

Chaud-froid
Poultry, or sometimes game,
served cold in aspic or glazed
with mayonnaise.

Chaudrée
Eel and potato stew with white
wine, from Poitou-Charentes.

Chavanne
Chub. Freshwater fish, bony and
slightly soft-fleshed. Sometimes
used in stews.

Celeriac may not look pretty, but it is used to great effect in French cooking.

Chavignol
Round goats' milk cheese from
Sancerre, sometimes known
as Crottin.

Chester
Brand name of a type of French
cheese that is similar to the
English Cheshire.

Chevaine or chevesne
Chub (see *chavanne*).

Cheval
Horse (meat).

Cheveux d'ange
Vermicelli.

Chèvre or chevreau
Goat.

Chevrette
Shrimp.

Chevreuil
Venison. Increasingly popular for its
tender and low-fat meat.

Chevru
Round cheese similar to Brie from
the Île-de-France.

Chicon
Chicory

Chicorée or frisée
Curly endive.

Chipiron
Basque name for squid.

Chocart or choquart
Apple pastry flavoured with spice
and lemon, from Brittany.

Chocolat
Chocolate. *Un chocolat* is a cup of
hot chocolate.

Chorizo
Spanish-style highly seasoned
sausage found in the South of
France. Used sometimes in
couscous (see recipe, pages
140–41).

Choron, sauce
Béarnaise sauce coloured with
tomato purée.

Chotenn bigoudenn
Roast pig's head with garlic.

Chou
Cabbage.

Choucroute
Sauerkraut.

Chou-fleur
Cauliflower.

Choumarin/chou de mer
Seakale.

Chou-navet
Swede.

Chou-rave
Kohlrabi.

Choux brocolis
Broccoli.

Choux de Bruxelles
Brussels sprouts.

Ciboule
Spring onion.

Ciboulettes or cives
Chives.

Citron
Lemon (*limon* is lime, not lemon).

Citrouille
Pumpkin.

Civet
A thick stew, thickened by using the
blood of the animal.

Civet de lièvre
Jugged hare.

Clafoutis
Classic baked batter pudding
made with cherries that comes
originally from Limousin (see
recipe, page 146).

Clamart
Served with artichoke hearts filled
with peas.

Claquebitou
Herb-flavoured goats' milk cheese
from Burgundy.

Clavelado
Another name for *raie* (ray or skate).

Clou de girofle
A clove.

Cochon de lait
Suckling pig.

Coco
Coconut.

Cocotte, en
Slow-cooked in a sealed pot or
heavy, lidded saucepan.

Coeur
Heart.

Coeur à la crème
Cream cheese served with sugar.

Coeur de filet
Prime cut of beef.

Coing
Quince.

Colimaçon
Snail.

Colin
Hake.

Colineau
Codling.

Colombière
Mild, smooth dish-shaped
cheese made with cows' milk,
from Savoie.

Compote
Stewed fruit.

Concombre
Cucumber.

Confit
Preserve, usually of fruit, in sugar.

Confit d'oie, de canard, de porc
Goose, duck or pork preserved in its own fat.

Confiture
Jam.

Congre
Conger eel.

Consommé
Clear soup.

Consommé julienne
Clear soup with thin strips of onion, turnip, celery etc.

Consommé madrilène
A clear meat soup flavoured with tomato juice.

Contre-filet
Beef sirloin fillet.

Coq
Cockerel.

Coq au vin
Chicken cooked in red wine with glazed shallots or small onions and button mushrooms.

Coq au vin jaune
An Arbois chicken dish, cooked in white wine, cream and morels.

Coq de bruyère
Grouse.

Coque, à la
Cooked in the shell, eg *oeuf à la coq* (boiled egg).

Coquillages
Shellfish.

Coquille St-Jacques
Scallop. Often cooked with cheese sauce or a white wine and cream sauce and served in its shell (see recipe, page 138).

Corne
A type of *brioche* from Nantes.

Corne grecque
Okra or lady's fingers.

Cornichon
Gherkin.

Côte
Rib, chop.

Côtelette
Chop or cutlet, usually lamb.

Cotignac
Quince paste. Eaten as a sweet.

Cotriade
Breton stew from a mixture of fish with onions, potatoes and cream.

Cou
Neck.

Coudenat
Pork sausage from southwest France. Eaten hot, in slices.

Couhé-Vérac
Goats' milk cheese from Poitou, served wrapped in chestnut leaves.

Coulis
Thick purée, often tomato, also made from fruit. Served as a sauce.

Coulommiers
Creamy-centred, disc-shaped cheese from Coulommiers in the Île-de-France.

43

Coupe Jacques
Strawberry and lemon ice-cream topped with fruit in kirsch.

Courge
Squash, gourd.

Courge à la moelle
Vegetable marrow.

Couronne de côtelettes rôtie
Roast crown of lamb.

Court-bouillon
Stock of herbs, vegetables and white wine used for poaching fish or in fish dishes.

Couscous
Cooked, rolled grains of semolina, steamed over a stew of vegetables, chicken and lamb served with *harissa* sauce – a hot, spicy condiment. A dish originally from North Africa served in many cafés and brasseries through France (see recipe, pages 140–41).

Coussinet
Cranberry.

Crabe
Crab.

Crabe froide à l'anglaise
Dressed crab.

Crécy, à la`
Soup featuring carrots.

Crème
Cream (see box, opposite)

Crêpe
Thin pancake, which may be sweet or savoury.

Crêpe dentelle
Very thin pancake from Brittany.

Crêpe Suzette
Dessert pancake flamed in Cointreau with orange sauce.

Crépinette
Small flat sausage wrapped in caul, from the Bordeaux area. Often served with oysters.

French fruit tartlets, such as these for sale at a Paris patisserie, are not to be missed.

CREAM AND CREAMY CONCOCTIONS

Although *crème* means cream and dishes *à la crème* have cream in them, the term is also used for custard mixtures that are not necessarily made with cream. Here is a run through of the main examples.

Crème, à la With cream, in a cream sauce.

Crème anglaise Custard.

Crème au beurre French butter cream, enriched with egg yolks and very sweet.

Crème brûlée Creamy egg custard with crisp topping of burnt sugar.

Crème caramel Set egg custard, turned out with caramel topping.

Crème Chantilly Sweetened whipped cream.

Crème fouettée Whipped cream.

Crème fraîche Fresh, slightly soured cream.

Crème à la vanille Egg custard flavoured with vanilla.

Crème pâtissière Confectioner's custard. A thick custard enriched with cream, used for filling tarts, pastries and gâteaux.

Cresson
Watercress.

Crevette
Shrimp, prawn.

Crevette grise
Shrimp.

Crevette rose
Prawn.

Crevette rouge
Large red prawn.

Croissant
Flaky breakfast crescent made in the same way as puff pastry, only with yeast dough and butter. The layers resemble puff pastry but the dough should be slightly more substantial – slightly bread-like. Generally eaten with *confiture*.

Croquant
Crunchy. Also name for types of *petit four* and honey biscuits.

Croque au sel
Eaten raw, with salt.

Croque-madame
Toasted ham and cheese sandwich with fried egg.

Croque–monsieur
Toasted cheese and ham sandwich.

Croquette
Fried meat-cake or fish-cake, coated in breadcrumbs.

Crottin
Small disc-shaped goats' milk cheese from the Loire. A name that appears increasingly on the menu. Often served grilled as a starter,

sometimes arranged on a bed of green salad.

Croupion
'Parson's nose' of chicken or other poultry.

Croustade
Casing of fried bread, or pastry.

Croustille
Snack of fried potato slices.

Croûte
Crust of bread as a base, or a pastry base.

Croûtons
Tiny squares of fried or toasted bread. Used as garnish for soup and added to warm salads.

Cruchades
Sweet cornmeal fritters from southwest France.

Crudités, assiette de
Raw young vegetables usually served with a delicious dip of garlic-flavoured mayonnaise. Vegetables include strips of carrot, turnip, pepper, cucumber and celery with cauliflower florets, radishes, spring onions, broad beans and tomatoes.

Crustacé
Shellfish, for example, lobster, crayfish, prawn.

Cuisse
Thigh.

Cuisse de poulet
Drumstick of chicken.

Cuisseau
Leg of veal.

Cuisses de grenouilles
Frogs' legs. Tasting much like chicken, they are usually sautéed with garlic or served with a cream sauce.

Cuit
Cooked: for example, steak *bien cuit* (well-done).

Cul
Chump chop.

Culotte
Rump steak of beef.

D

Dariole
Form of cream pastry, or custard, that is cooked in a small bucket-shaped mould.

Darne
Thick fish steak.

Datte
Date.

Daube
Meat, usually beef, braised slowly in red wine, herbs, carrots and onions. A Provençal *daube* often has orange peel included. By tradition the *daube* is cooked overnight in a closed pot over a slow fire.

Dauphinoise, à la
Usually potatoes sliced and baked in milk. It makes a very filling accompaniment to any meal or, sprinkled with cheese, can be served as a lunch dish.

Frogs' legs are a delicious French dish, with a flavour similar to chicken.

Daurade
Sea bream.

Demi-sel
Slightly salted cream cheese.

Diable
Usually kidneys or *poussins*, which are split, flattened, then grilled and served with hot pepper and a vinegar sauce.

Dieppoise, à la
Fish, often sole, cooked the Dieppe way in white wine sauce, garnished with shellfish. Some of the best seafood in the world is from the Dieppe area.

Dijonnais
Meat, or poultry, often rabbit or chicken, cooked with mustard sauce. It is important that the mustard used is the Dijon variety, not the fiercer types.

Dinde or dindon
Turkey. Not eaten as much in France as it is in Britain and the US, but found in country areas such as the Dordogne.

Diot
Pork and vegetable sausage from Savoie, usually in white wine.

Dorade
Sea bream.

Dorée
John Dory (fish).

Dur
Hard, eg *oeuf dur* (a hard-boiled egg).

Duxelles
A savoury mix of mushrooms and shallots cooked in butter until they virtually become a paste. Used as a base for some sauces and casseroles.

E

Écarlate
Salted, pickled meat, usually tongue. Sometimes on sale in *traiteurs* or *charcuteries* (see pages 125–6).

Échalote
Shallot. A mild, more elegant form of onion, used extensively in French cookery. It gives a more subtle taste to casseroles, sauces and other dishes than the onion does.

Échine
Chine, loin of pork.

Échourgnac
Small, yellow-rinded cheese with holes in it, from Périgord.

Écrevisse
Freshwater crayfish with a delicious, slightly sweet taste. Although France's many freshwater rivers, streams and lakes have always yielded a rich harvest of crayfish, a virus is now affecting availability.

Églefin
Haddock.

Émincé
Thinly sliced. Slivers of meat or poultry reheated in sauce. Many people misread this word on the menu and reject it, thinking they are going to be presented with mince.

Emmenthal
Large wheel-shaped cheese with a honeycomb texture and slightly sweet taste that is similar to, and usually cheaper than, Gruyère. You can use it with great success in a fondue, for instance.

Enchaud
Baked garlic-flavoured pork and pigs' trotters with truffles from Périgord, a real country dish.

Encornet
Squid.

Encre
Black ink of octopus or squid. Often used in Mediterranean seafood dishes.

Endive
Chicory, the slightly bitter vegetable with long leaves of pale yellow packed close together. Used raw in salads or braised (*endives à l'étuvée*). *Endives au jambon* are braised heads of chicory wrapped in ham.

Entremets
Sweets.

Épaule
Shoulder, usually of lamb (*épaule d'agneau*).

Épice
Spice.

Épinards
Spinach.

Époisses
Flat cylindrical cheese from Burgundy. Made from cows' milk, it has an orange-red rind that develops from being washed in *marc* (grape-must brandy).

Escalope

Flattened slice of veal or poultry breast, often served fried.

Escalope à la viennoise

Veal dipped in egg and breadcrumbs, then sautéed. Although this is not a French but an Italian dish, it appears very often on the cheaper tourist menus.

Escalope normande Vallée d'Auge

Veal or chicken breast served with cream, Calvados and apple. A delicious but very rich dish from Normandy.

Escargot

Snail. The best snails are said to come from Burgundy, but now they are being imported from various other countries including Turkey and even England. Snails have very little flavour and a slightly rubbery texture – they are rather like whelks or winkles.

Escargots à la bourguignonne

Snails stuffed with garlic butter and parsley.

Escarole

An extra curly-leaved form of endive.

Espadon

Swordfish. This has a rather dry, meat-like texture but is very good grilled, served with melted butter.

Espagnole, sauce

A brown sauce made with bacon, carrots, onions, wine, herbs and spices. Served with meat or pasta.

Esprot

Sprat.

Esquinade

Spider crab.

Estouffade

Basically a pot-roasted steak. Meat, usually beef, often cooked in one steak rather than cut into pieces, braised slowly and for a long time in a closed pot until very tender.

Estragon

Tarragon.

Exocet (poisson volant)

Flying fish, with fins that resemble wings and the ability to skim above water. The flesh is flavoursome and often treated as mackerel.

F

Faisan, faisandeau or faisane

Pheasant. It is served fairly widely in France. Roast pheasant (*faisan rôti*), stewed pheasant (*faisan en cocotte*) and other local styles of cooking are used.

Far

Rum-flavoured flan or tart with an ancient name, which comes from Brittany.

Farce, farci

Stuffing, stuffed.

Farci niçois

A chic form of *ratatouille*. Stuffed courgettes, aubergines (eggplants), tomatoes and onions, cooked slowly in olive oil.

Farine
Flour.

Faséole
Kidney bean.

Faux-filet
Piece of beef sirloin.

Faverolles
A name given to haricot beans in the South of France. They are used in local dishes such as *cassoulet*.

Fechun
Pork-stuffed cabbage, a hearty dish from the Franche-Comté area, near the German border.

Fenouil
Fennel. A vegetable that is used extensively in France. It has a distinctive aniseed taste.

Ferchuse
Pork offal, cooked in red wine with potatoes and onions, from Burgundy. Traditionally the heart and lungs form the main part of the dish.

Fermière, à la
Meat, sometimes chicken, braised with mixed vegetables.

Fève
Broad bean.

Ficelle
Very thin *baguette*.

Ficelle Picarde
Pancake rolled round a filling of ham and mushrooms, then baked with cream and cheese.

Figue
Fig. Raw green figs make a delicious dessert, served in summer in the south. Sometimes eaten as a starter with ham.

Filet mignon
Small fillet steak.

Cans of foie gras, *a rich and expensive French delicacy.*

Fines herbes

Finely chopped herbs. Used for flavouring, particularly omelettes. Usually parsley, chervil, tarragon and chives.

Flageolet

Small bean. Oval in shape and pale green, they are often served with lamb.

Flamande

In the Flemish way. A hearty meal of meat with braised root vegetables, cabbage and bacon.

Flambé

Flamed in brandy or some other spirit, often done to steak or pancakes. A practice that is now confined to the more old-fashioned establishments.

Flan

A sweet or savoury flan of the quiche variety. The name is also often used, particularly in the south, for a rather heavy type of egg custard, a less delicate version of *crème caramel*.

Flétan

Halibut.

Flondre

Flounder.

Florentine, á la

Cooked or served with spinach, sometimes with cheese sauce. It is also the name for small chocolate-coated biscuits.

Foie

Liver.

Foie gras

'Fat liver' of goose or duck. *Pâté de foie gras* sometimes has truffles added, a speciality of the Landes district. The birds are force-fed with grain so that their livers become enlarged to produce the *foie* in large quantities. Graphic pictures of the process, on hoardings by the roadside, tend to put visitors off the product rather than encouraging them to buy it.

Fond

Base, eg *fond d'artichaut*, the part that is eaten last, once the leaves have been drained of their goodness. Sometimes *fond d'artichaut* is served *clamart*, with a little heap of peas in the middle, as a garnish for a dish.

Fondu au marc

Sometimes called *fondu aux raisins*, a type of processed cheese from Savoie. Sold in discs, it is covered with a distinctive rind of grape pips.

Fondue

Pot of hot, molten Gruyère cheese, white wine and kirsch, from Savoie. Cubes of bread are used for dipping.

Fondue bourguignonne

Pieces of steak cooked on forks in boiling oil with a variety of flavoured sauces to accompany them. The meat must be of top quality. The sauces range from curry-flavoured mayonnaise to tomato sauce. The dish came originally from Burgundy, and is frequently served in ski resorts.

Foudjou

Strong goats' milk cheese with brandy and garlic, and served with potatoes. This makes an extremely pungent meal. From the Languedoc.

Fougasse

A type of bread, sometimes pastry (varies according to region). The *fougasse* of Provence resembles the leaf of a Swiss-cheese plant, with its network of large holes.

Four, au

Baked in the oven, sometimes roasted.

Fourme

Name given to a number of cheeses from Auvergne made from cows' milk. Fourme d'Ambert is a cylindrical blue-veined cheese. Fourme de Montbrison, sometimes called Fourme de Cantal, has a sharper taste.

Frais

Fresh, cool.

Fraise

Strawberry.

Fraises des bois

Wild strawberries. They are tiny and have a delicious, perfumed, sweet flavour. Often served as a dessert.

Fraises Romanoff

A dish of fresh strawberries soaked in liqueur and orange juice, with whipped cream on top. Very easy to prepare.

Framboise

Raspberry.

Frangipane

Almond-flavoured confectioner's custard. Used in cakes and gâteaux and, occasionally, as a lining to a *tarte*, a buffer between the pastry and the topping. It looks rather like egg custard and tastes strongly of vanilla.

Frappé

Iced, served on crushed ice.

Frappo

Casseroled ox tripe from the Languedoc. Not a dish to tackle unless you are extremely hungry.

Fréchure

Casserole of pigs' lungs, from Vivarais.

Fressure

Pig or calf offal, used extensively in French country cooking.

Friandise

Petit four, sweet.

Fricassée

Chopped white meat, ie veal or chicken, cooked in cream sauce.

Fricaude

Stew of pigs' offal from the Lyonnais.

Frisée

Curly, such as the leaves of endive, parsley.

Frit

Fried.

Juicy strawberries find a good home in a range of French desserts, cakes and drinks.

Frites
Chips. Frequently sold on camp-sites and at roadside stalls.

Friture
A pile of fried food, usually small fish.

Froid
Cold.

Fromage
Cheese. France has hundreds, and the best ones are those given an AOC (*Appellation d'Origine Contrôlée*), just like wines. See The Regions of France (pages 10–27) for descriptions of many local cheeses. Also see under individual cheeses in this A–Z listing.

Fromage à la croûte
The French equivalent of Welsh rarebit (toasted cheese) using slices of rather soft bread.

Fromage de tête
'Head cheese', or brawn.

Fromage d'Italie
Not a cheese but something very different – a dish made with pig's liver.

Fromage du curé
Cows' milk cheese from the Nantes area. It is square and has a strong smell.

Fromaget
Cheesecake.

Fruit de mer
Shellfish. The plural, *fruits de mer*, usually means a plate piled high with a selection of shellfish including, if you are lucky, oysters, prawns and even lobster. It comes accompanied by instruments for extracting meat out of lobsters' claws, for cracking shells and so on.

Fumé
Smoked.
Fumet
Strong fish stock.

G

Galantine
Meat or poultry, usually stuffed, poached and pressed in aspic. Eaten as a first course or as part of an *hors d'oeuvre*. It is also the name of a type of cheese from northern France.

Galette
A pancake made with buckwheat flour (*sarrasin*), a Breton speciality. The batter is spread on a hot griddle, using a special wooden scraper, until it is thin and even. The flipped cooked pancake usually has a savoury filling. A speciality is to top the *galette* with ham and an egg. The pancake is then folded and served at once. *Galettes* are widely available at *crêperies* throughout France.

Galette de la Chaise-Dieu
Not a pancake but a cheese that comes from Auvergne. Unusually for this area, it is made from goats' milk and is very slightly sweet.

Gamba
Large prawn.

Gaperon
Dome-shaped cheese from Auvergne, made from cows' milk, spiked with garlic and black pepper.

Garbure
A soup or stew made from mixed vegetables, mainly root varieties, served with beans and bacon.

A shellfish stall in Paris offers wine to complement your meal.

Originating in Gascony, it is found all over France.

Gâteau
Sponge cake or tart, sweet or sometimes savoury.

Gâteau au fromage
Cheesecake. Although the French do not have a passion for this particular dessert, it is becoming increasingly popular.

Gaufre, gaufrette
Water biscuit or waffle.

Gelée, en
In aspic.

Genièvre
Juniper. The berries are used in many savoury dishes from the Ardennes, and some *apéritifs* too.

Génoise
Sponge cake.

Gésiers
Preserved poultry gizzards or giblets, often served in salads.

Gex, Bleu de
A firm blue-veined cows' milk cheese of flat cylindrical shape from the Haut-Jura. Once made in huts on the mountain slopes, it is now manufactured in modern dairies.

Gibier
Game.

Gien
A cows' milk cheese from the Loire valley, cured in wood ash.

Gigoret
Pig's head cooked in blood and red wine, a dish from Poitou-Charentes.

Gigot
Leg of lamb, occasionally goat.

Gigot pourri
Lamb cooked with whole cloves of garlic, a dish from Rouergue.

Gingembre
Ginger.

Girofle
Clove (spice).

Gîte à la noix
Beef silverside.

Glace
Ice, ice-cream.

Glace au café
Coffee ice-cream, as opposed to *café glacé*, iced coffee.

Gougère
A delicious light cheese-flavoured choux pastry bun or ring from Burgundy.

Goujons
Small strips of fish or chicken, coated in breadcrumbs and deep-fried.

Gourmandise
Sweetmeat.

Gournay
A cows' milk cheese from the town of the same name in Normandy. It is soft, salty and comes in a flat disc shape.

Gousse d'ail
Clove of garlic.

Goûter
To taste.

Goyave
Guava.

Grain de cassis
Blackcurrant.

Granité
Type of crunchy water ice.

Gratin
A dish with a crust of browned breadcrumbs, possibly mixed with cheese.

Gratin dauphinois
Potato slices baked in milk and sometimes cheese (see recipe, pages 135–6).

Grattons
Fried cubed pork and pork fat.

Grecque, à la
Southern vegetable dish that contains mushrooms, aubergines (eggplants) or other variations, poached in oil and herbs, then served hot or cold.

Grenade
Pomegranate.

Grenadin
Thick slice of veal; the term is also sometimes applied to other meat.

Grenouille
Frog. (See *cuisses de grenouille*.)

Grignaudes
Fried pieces of pork, from Berry. Rather like *rillons*, they are usually eaten cold.

Grillade
Grill, of steak, lamb chop etc.

Grillade au fenouil
Fish, usually mullet or sea bass, grilled over sprigs of fennel often over a barbecue, a dish of Provence.

Griotte
Bitter cherry.

Gris de Lille
A very salty, strong-smelling cheese from the north of France. Made from cows' milk, it is recognisable by its distinctive square shape and sticky pinkish-grey rind.

Grive
Thrush, now banned as food under EC regulations. Sometimes still found as canned pâté.

Gros mollet
Lumpfish.

Groseille
Redcurrant, white currant.

Groseille à maquereau
Gooseberry.

Groseille de cheval
Cranberry.

Gruyère
Both the French and the Swiss lay claim to this cheese and, under a court decision made in 1951, both countries are allowed to call their product by this name. The two best-known French versions are Gruyère de Comté, made in the Franche-Comté region, and Beaufort, which has no holes in it. (The French also make Emmenthal, which used to be considered a type of Gruyère but is now classed as a separate cheese.)

H

Hachis parmentier
The French equivalent of shepherd's pie: minced lamb topped with mashed potato.

Halicot or haricot de mouton
Stewed mutton with root vegetables but rarely haricot beans.

Hareng
Herring.

Harissa
A fiery North African paste of red chillies and spices. Buy it in tubes or jars to serve with couscous.

Hochepot
A filling soup of beef, mutton, salt pork, pigs' ears and tail, cabbage and root vegetables.

Hollandaise
Hot or warm sauce made from butter, wine and lemon juice, thickened with egg yolks.

Homard
Lobster.

Homard à l'armoricaine/ l'américaine
Lobster served with a sauce of brandy, white wine, onions, tomatoes and herbs. A dish that comes from Brittany and is found mainly in the north of France.

Homard thermidor
Sautéed lobster cooked in a creamy white wine sauce, topped with Parmesan cheese then browned under the grill.

Hors d'oeuvre
Mixture (usually cold) of meat, fish and vegetable dishes served as an appetiser.

Huître
Oyster. On a menu, the type and/ or origin may well be specified, and the size should be as well, with size 06 being the smallest and 00 the largest.

I

Igny
A mild disc-shaped cheese from the Champagne area. It is made from cows' milk by the monks at the Abbey of Igny in the Marne region.

Île flottante
A favourite French pudding, islands of whipped egg white poached in (and floating in) custard and drizzled with caramelised sugar.

Indienne, à l'
With a curry-flavoured sauce, usually a mild one.

Iraty
A strong cheese containing a mix of cows' milk from the Basque country. The cheese varies in its pungency from season to season, according to how much ewes' milk is included.

Italienne, à l'
Served with pasta, mushrooms and tomato.

REGIONAL HAMS

Many different parts of France have their own special hams – from the area around Toulouse, for instance, from the Jura, from Morlaix in Brittany and from the Ardennes. The most famous ham of all is probably the mild cured *Jambon de Bayonne*, which is sold all over France. *Jambon cru* is raw, often wind-dried, ham. *Jambon de Paris* is a name for ordinary cooked ham. *Jambon fumé* is smoked ham, while *Jambonneau* is a small ham, usually a knuckle bone. *Jambon persillé* is ham that is usually cubed, then preserved *Bourgogne*-style with parsley in a type of wine jelly. *Jambonnette* refers to dry salt pork sausage shaped to look like a ham, and comes from the Vivarois area.

J

Jambon, jambonneau
Ham (see box, above).

Jonchée
Delicious fresh cream cheese from Poitou-Charentes. The name is also used in other parts of France – the Loire and Brittany, for instance – to refer to a type of junket (a milky dessert).

Joue
Cheek, usually of pork.

Julienne
Thin strips of vegetables, which are sometimes poached in butter, served as a garnish for a main dish.

Jus
Juice, gravy.

K

Kig-ha-farz
Breton pork and vegetable buckwheat dumpling.

Knackwurst
Frankfurter-type sausage from Alsace.

Kougelhopf
Fluted *brioche* ring, studded with nuts and dried raisins, from Alsace.

L

Laguiole
One of the great AOC cheeses from the Aubrac area. It has a strong herb flavour as it is made with milk from cows raised on land with thyme, fennel and other pungent plants growing on it.

Lait
Milk.

Laitue
Lettuce.

Landaise, à la
Cooked in goose fat with garlic and pine kernels, from the Landes area in the southwest.

Langouste
Spiny lobster, sea crayfish.

Langoustine
Dublin bay prawn, large scampi.

Langres
A tall, disc-shaped cheese with a dip in the top and a moist orange rind that is washed in champagne or *marc de Champagne*.

Langue or languette
Tongue.

Langue de chat
Long thin biscuit.

Languier
Smoked pork tongue.

Lapin or lapereau
Rabbit.

Laqueuille, Bleu de
A strong, soft blue cheese, very like Roquefort, from the Auvergne.

Lardons
Small cubes or sticks of bacon, which are often used to garnish dishes as well as in salads.

Laruns
A cheese made from ewes' milk that comes from the Basque country.

Légumes
Vegetables.

Lentille
Lentil.

France is a real haven for lovers of seafood.

Levroux
A strong-smelling but mild cheese from the Loire made from goats' milk, similar to Valençay.

Lièvre
Hare. *Civet de lièvre* is jugged hare.

Ligueil
A cylindrical goats' milk cheese from the Loire valley with a strong flavour.

Limande
Dab (fish). *Sole limande* is lemon sole.

Limon
Lime.

Livarot
Small, pungent, disc-shaped cheese from Normandy, made from cows' milk.

Lormes
A cone-shaped goats' milk cheese from the Nivernais.

Lotte de mer
Monkfish.

Loudes, Bleu de
Yet another blue-veined cheese from the Massif Central. This one, which is made from cows' milk, comes from the Le Puy area.

Loukinka
Spicy garlic sausage from the Basque country.

Loup de mer
Sea bass. Served in the south of France grilled on fennel twigs, often flamed in Pernod (*loup grillé au fenouil*).

Lusignan
A fresh cheese from the Poitou area made from goats' milk, sometimes used in cheesecakes.

Lyonnaise, à la
Cooked with onions, Lyon-style. This term usually refers to potatoes, but is sometimes also used for liver.

M

Macédoine
Mixture of diced fruit or vegetables, used either in a salad or *hors d'oeuvre* or as a dessert.

Mâche
Corn salad, lamb's lettuce. A small-leafed, winter variety of lettuce with tender dark green leaves that have a mild, buttery lettuce flavour.

Madeleine
Small conical sponge cake.

Magnum
A rich, creamy disc-shaped cheese from Normandy, which is similar to Brillat-Savarin.

Maigre
Lean.

Maigret/magret
Grilled breast of duck, usually served sliced and rare.

Maïs
Sweetcorn.

Maquereau
Mackerel.

Maquereau au vin blanc
Mackerel cooked in white wine. Often served cold as a first course in northern France.

Marbrade
Pig's head in aspic, a dish from southwest France.

Marcassin
Young wild boar.

Marchand de vin
Meat, usually steak, with red wine and shallots.

Marmande
The large, ridged tomato of the south.

Marmite
The name of a tall stewing pot, as well as that of dishes cooked in it, such as *marmite dieppoise*, a fish stew with leeks, cream and white wine.

Maroilles
One of the AOC cheeses of France that comes from Flanders. It is also one of the oldest cheeses, said to have been invented by monks at the abbey there over 1,000 years ago. Do not be put off by its pungent smell; it tastes delicious, if a trifle spicy. It is often used in *tartes* in the north of France.

Marron
Chestnut.

Marrons glacés
Chestnuts preserved and glazed in sugar.

Massepain
Marzipan, or sometimes a cake made with almond paste.

Matefaim
Type of thick pancake or batter pudding from Berry. It can be sweet or savoury.

Matelote
Casserole of freshwater fish with onions, mushrooms and wine.

Méchoui
Barbecued lamb, North African-style, often with cumin. Found in Paris or in the south – anywhere where there is an Arab population of any size.

Médaillon
Small round fillet steak.

Mélange
Blend or mixture.

Menthe
Mint, mint-flavoured.

Merguez
A popular spicy sausage of Spanish origins, served grilled.

Merlan
Whiting.

Merluche
Hake, salted or fresh.

Mesclun
Mixed green salad from Provence. Now sold bagged in supermarkets.

Meunière, à la
Flour-coated and fried or grilled with butter, lemon juice and parsley.

Miel
Honey.

Mignonnette
Small round fillet of lamb.

Mignot
A Normandy cheese very similar to the famous Livarot.

Mille-feuille
Flaky pastry slices sandwiched with jam and cream.

Minute
Flash-cooked steak or sometimes sole, grilled or fried.

Mirabelle
Small yellow plum.

Mirepoix
Diced root vegetable and bacon mix, cooked in butter. Forms the basis of several sauces.

Mirliton
Little pastry cakes featuring ground almonds, from Rouen.

Mode, à la
Marinated meat, usually beef, braised in wine with calf's foot, bacon and vegetables.

Mollet
Soft, soft-boiled, as for eggs.

Monsieur
A firm and fruity Normandy cheese made from cows' milk. It has a red-spotted rind and a strong smell.

Mont-Blanc
Chestnut purée that is pushed through a sieve or mincer and topped with whipped cream to resemble the mountain – Europe's highest.

Montoire
A delicious mild goats' milk cheese from the Loire valley.

French honey – miel – on sale at a specialist honey shop in Paris.

Montrachet
A creamy cylindrical goats' milk cheese. It is sold wrapped in chestnut or, sometimes, in vine leaves.

Montségur
A cows' milk cheese from Languedoc-Roussillon with a very mild, bland flavour.

Morbier
A strong-flavoured cows' milk cheese from the Jura. Easily identified because it has a black streak of ash running through the centre.

Morceau
A small morsel, tiny portion.

Morille/morel
A type of wild mushroom that is rare and expensive. Dark brown to black in colour, with a honeycomb-textured cap, this variety needs thorough washing and long cooking. They are springtime mushrooms and are also sold dried. Pale morels are cheaper because they do not have as good a flavour.

Mornay
With a cheese sauce.

Morue
Cod, sometimes dried or more usually salted. It is used to make *brandade*.

Moules
Mussels, *Moules farcies* are stuffed mussels.

Moules à la marinière
Mussels cooked in a thin shallot and white wine sauce.

Mousse
Light mixture, a type of cold soufflé.

Mousseline
With whipped cream or egg white.

Moutarde
Mustard. The best mustards are considered to come from Dijon, Meaux and Reims.

Mouton
Mutton.

Mulet
Grey Mullet.

Munster
One of France's AOC cheeses, a pungent disc-shaped cheese that has a dark red skin, from Alsace. It looks soft and mild but actually has a very strong flavour and smell, and it is something of an acquired taste. You will sometimes find it sold with a cumin seed flavouring, which gives it an aniseed tang.

Mûre
Blackberry.

Mûre de mûrier
Mulberry.

Mûre de ronce
Blackberry.

Murol
A mild cows' milk cheese from the town of the same name in the Auvergne. It is similar in

flavour to the better-known
St-Nectaire.

Myrtille
Bilberry.

N

Nantua
Denotes a fish dish, often sole,
that is garnished with freshwater
crayfish tails.

Nature
Plain, as in, for example, *omelette
nature*. The term is also used to
refer to coffee or tea that is served
without milk.

Navarin
A simple lamb stew with onions
and potatoes.

Navet
Turnip.

Négresse en chemise
A very popular French pudding of
chocolate ice-cream or mousse
served like a sandcastle, with a
'moat' of cream round the edge.

Neufchâtel
One of the great AOC cheeses
called after the town of the same
name in Normandy. It is usually
sold or served on a bed of straw,
and it comes in many shapes
from cylindrical to heart-shaped.
You may also find it sold under
the name of Bondon. It has a
white rind, a soft texture and a
milky flavour.

Niçoise, à la
Meaning Nice-fashion, this usually
refers to a dish that relies heavily
on the use of tomatoes, garlic,
anchovies, olives and, probably,
aubergines (eggplants).

Noisette
Nut, hazelnut. Sometimes refers
to a small cake topped with
hazelnuts.

**Noisette/noix d'agneau, boeuf,
veau**
A small round cut of meat – lamb,
beef, veal.

Noix
Nut, walnut.

Normande, à la
Meat or poultry cooked Normandy-
style, that is, with apples, cream
and cider or Calvados. If it
refers to fish, it is usually served
with a simple white wine and
cream sauce.

Nougat
A soft chewy sweet containing
nuts and honey from Montélimar.
Although nougat is now made
everywhere, Montélimar is
especially renowned for this
confection and it is worth taking
some home with you. It is
usually sold cut up into squares
or bars.

Nouilles
Noodles.

O

Oeuf

Egg. *Oeuf brouillé* is scrambled egg, *oeuf à la coque* is an egg that is soft-boiled in its shell. Hard-boiled egg is *oeuf dur* and *oeuf en cocotte* is egg cooked in a small ramekin. *Oeuf frit* or *oeuf à la poêle* means fried egg, while *oeuf mollet* is an egg that is soft-boiled and shelled. Poached egg is *oeuf poché* and *oeuf sur le plat* refers to egg baked in butter.

Oie/oison

Goose, a favourite choice on the menu in the Dordogne/Landes area of France, also in Alsace.

Oignon

Onion.

Oiseau sans tête

Not a small headless bird, as you might imagine, but stuffed, rolled fillet of beef.

Oléron

A cheese from the Île d'Oléron off the Charantes coast, made, as are many cheeses in this area, from ewes' milk. Of no particular shape, it has a mild creamy flavour.

Olive

Olive. Most French olives are grown in Provence. Green olives are unripe and black olives ripe fruit. The wrinkled versions have been left on the trees a long time before picking. Olives are preserved in brine or oil and may be flavoured with garlic, herbs or spices, or stuffed with pimento or nuts.

Olivet Bleu

A blue-veined cheese from the Orléans area made from cows' milk and matured in caves. It has a pleasant, fairly mild taste.

Olivet cendré

A similar cheese to Olivet Bleu, from the same area. Cured in wood ash, it has a slightly firmer texture and more pronounced flavour.

Omelette

Omelette. Served in both sweet and savoury ways in France (see box, page 67).

Oreille or oreillette

Ear of pig, used quite often in country dishes.

Orrys, les

A mountain cheese from the Languedoc-Roussillon area, made from cows' milk. It is hard in texture and strong-tasting, and comes in large flat discs. Often used in place of Parmesan for grating over food.

Os, à l'

With bone marrow, which is used for flavouring sauces and stews.

Ouillade

Pungent garlic-flavoured bean and vegetable soup from the Languedoc area.

Oursin

Sea urchin. Sometimes found in dishes of *fruits de mer*.

P

Paillette dorée
Cheese straw.

Paillettes d'oignons frits
Fried crisp onion rings.

Pain
Bread. For more information on the variety of breads, see page 125.

Pain au chocolat
Rectangular croissant with a strip of chocolate in the middle. Best eaten warm.

Palombe
Woodpigeon.

Palourde
Cockle or clam.

Pamplemousse
Grapefruit.

Pan bagna, bagnat
Baguette or roll that is stuffed with sliced tomatoes, onions, hard-boiled egg, strips of sweet pepper, olives and anchovies, and moistened with olive oil. From Provence.

Panaché
Mixed, as in *salade panachée*.

Panais
Parsnip.

Papillotte, en
Meat or fish cooked and served in a little packet of greased paper or foil.

Parfait
Frozen mousse or mousse-like cream, used in desserts, with a coffee, chocolate, vanilla or strawberry flavour.

Parmentier
A dish that contains potatoes. *Potage parmentier* is very similar to *vichyssoise*, but is a slightly less elegant leek and potato soup.

Passe-l'an
A hard cheese from the Languedoc, which, as its name implies ('passed the year'), is left to mature for a least one year – probably two. It is sold in segments from enormous flat discs, and is often grated over food.

Passe-pierre
Samphire. A fleshy plant that grows between shoreline rocks (the name means 'pass through stone'). Also called *salicorne*. Served, fresh or pickled, with fish dishes or used to garnish *fruits de mer*.

Patate
Sweet potato.

Pâte
This word can mean either pastry or pasta, according to what is associated with it. *Pâte brisée* is shortcrust pastry, *pâte à chou* is choux pastry, and *pâte feuilletée* is flaky or puff pastry. The French also have *pâte sablée*, which is a form of rich shortcrust with sugar in it, used for tarts. *Pâte d'amandes* is marzipan and *pâte frollée* is almond-flavoured pastry.

Pâté
A cooked meat or fish paste, smooth or chunky, served cold.

A FRENCH CULINARY TREAT

Eating a good omelette is to experience classic, simple cooking at its best. Served perhaps with a salad, or some bread, it should be a meal to remember.

Omelette au jambon is an omelette with ham. *Omelette aux champignons* is a mushroom omelette; *aux fines herbes* is one with finely chopped herbs stirred in. *Omelette au fromage* is a cheese omelette, while *omelette nature* is a plain omelette. *À la confiture* is a sweet fluffy omelette with jam.

The phrase: 'I'll just have an omelette', does not apply in France: if you order one it will almost certainly contain at least four eggs.

Pâté de campagne
Coarse pâté, usually made from pork and almost certainly including garlic and other herbs.

Pâté de foie gras
Expensive goose or duck liver pâté, sometimes laced with truffles, which you can often buy canned.

Pâte de fruits
A fruit jelly.

Pâté en croûte
Pâté cooked in a pastry covering, rather like a game pie.

Pâté maison
This pâté is likely to be smooth and based on chicken or pig's liver.

Paupiette
Slice of meat, such as veal or beef, occasionally fish, which is rolled round a savoury filling.

Pavé d'Auge
A Normandy cheese with a strong taste yet a soft texture. It comes in squares and is golden yellow in colour.

Pavé
Meaning 'paving stone', this can apply to many square items of food, from gingerbread to a cut of meat.

Pays, de
Of the region.

Pêche
Peach.

Pélardons
A family of small soft goats' milk cheeses from the Cévennes. The name is also given to small cheeses cured in *marc* (local brandy), found in the Savoie region.

Perche
Freshwater perch.

Perdreau/perdrix
Partridge.

Périgourdine, à la
Served Périgord-style, with a garnish of truffles and *foie*

gras. Any such dish will be rich
and expensive.

Persil

Parsley.

Persillé

Served with parsley, or with a
parsley sauce.

Persillé

Name of a series of blue cheeses
from Savoie made from goats'
milk. Names to look for are Persillé
d'Aravis, Persillé de Thônes or
Persillé du Grand-Bornand – they
are all basically the same cheese.

Pet de nonne

Literally 'nun's fart', this is the local
name in Burgundy for a light soufflé
fritter, similar to a *beignet*.

Peteram

Sheep's trotter and tripe stew
from the Languedoc. To be avoided
by those who are timid about
eating offal.

Petit beurre

Small biscuit, made with butter.

Petit Bressan

A small cheese from the Lyonnaise.
It is made from cows' or goats'
milk, or a mixture of the two.

Petit four

Small after-dinner cake or biscuit,
usually served with coffee.

Petit-salé

Salt pork. Also a dish of salt pork
with lentils.

Petit-Suisse

Little pots of fresh, creamy unsalted
cheese, eaten with a spoon, often
with sugar sprinkled on top.

Petites

Tripe of sheep or veal from the
Languedoc.

There are many different types of delicious goats' milk cheeses to choose from.

Petits pois
Small sweet peas. Often served with baby cocktail-size onions. Very good bought canned.

Picodon
Generic name for a series of goats' milk cheeses from the Drôme-Rhône valley area.

Pièce de boeuf
Prime cut of beef.

Pied
Trotter, foot.

Pieds et paquets
Sheep tripe that is folded into packets, cooked with trotters, tomatoes and wine; a traditional Provençal dish that many find unexpectedly delicious.

Pigeon/pigeonneau
Pigeon.

Pignons
Pine nuts. These are used a great deal in Provençal cooking – in *soupe au pistou*, for instance, and in some dishes from the Landes area.

Pigouille
A creamy cheese from Charentais, near the Atlantic coast. It can be made from cows', goats' or ewes' milk and is usually sold wrapped in straw.

Piment
Green or red pepper.

Piment d'Esplette
Sun-dried red peppers with a spicy flavour, from the town on Esplette in the Pyrenees. Available powdered, crumbled, or as a paste. Used as a seasoning in many dishes of the region.

Piment doux
Sweet pepper.

Piment fort
Chilli, cayenne.

Pintade/pintadeau
Guinea fowl.

Pipérade
An egg dish that comes from the Basque country with onions, red peppers and tomatoes (see recipe, page 136).

Pissaladière
Type of yeast-dough tart, similar to pizza, which is covered with slow-cooked onions, anchovies and olives. Found everywhere in the South of France.

Pissenlit
Dandelion. The phrase literally means 'wet-the-bed'. Dandelion leaves are used in salads, particularly with a combination of other wild leaves.

Pistou
A sauce based on basil pounded with garlic, pine nuts and olive oil. Used, among other dishes, to flavour a Provençal soup. Similar to Italian *pesto*.

Pithiviers
Delicious flaky pastry gâteau, filled with *frangipane* (almond cream) and flavoured with rum. Named after a town in the Orléanais.

Pithiviers au foin
Not in fact a pastry, but a soft disc-shaped cheese from the Loire area, sold covered with strips of dried grass.

Plateau de fromages
Cheeseboard. In France they will certainly be fresh and include local cheeses.

Plateau de fruits de mer
Platter of seafood, usually laid out decoratively, often on crushed ice and garnished with seaweed. The best *plateaux* come from Normandy and Brittany.

Plie
Plaice.

Pochade
Stew of freshwater fish with raisins and carrots, from Savoie.

Poché
Poached.

Pochouse
Burgundian stew of eel and other freshwater fish in white wine with garlic.

Point, à
Medium, eg steak.

Pointe
Tip; for example, *pointe d'asperge* (asparagus tip).

Poire
Pear.

Poire de terre
Jerusalem artichoke.

Poireau
Leek.

Poirée
White beet, chard.

Poires Alma
Pears cooked in port.

Poires Belle-Hélène
Cooked pears with ice-cream and hot chocolate sauce.

Pois
Peas. Petits pois are little sweet green peas.

Pois chiches
Chickpeas. Used in dishes in the south.

Poisson
Fish.

Poisson volant
Flying fish.

Poitrine
Breast of lamb or veal.

Poivre d'Ane
A goats' milk cheese, well worth looking out for, from the hinterland of the Côte d'Azur. It has a distinctive herby flavour.

Poivron
Sweet pepper.

Pomme
Apple.

Pomme de terre
Potato. The words *de terre* are usually dispensed with, leaving it to your good sense to decide whether it is apple or potato you are getting (see box, opposite).

Pont-l'Évêque
Famous cows' milk cheese from the Normandy town of that name.

THE NOBLE POTATO

France is the place to sample many of the famous classic potato dishes at their best. However, for plain cooked potatoes, order *pommes vapeur*. If you want potatoes baked in their jackets ask for them *en robe de chambre*. New potatoes cooked slowly in butter over a gentle heat are *pommes fondantes* – golden soft and delicious.

Pommes allumettes Thin-cut chips.

Pommes Anna A dish of thinly sliced potatoes, oven-baked in butter.

Pommes dauphinoises Somewhat similar to *pommes Anna* but more moist – the potatoes are sliced, then oven-baked in milk.

Pommes duchesse Puréed potato piped decoratively on the plate.

Pommes frites, frites Chips.

Pommes Lyonnaises A delicious dish of potatoes sautéed with onion.

Pommes mousseline Soufflé potatoes – sometimes puréed with beaten egg white, nowadays more often with cream.

Pommes paillées Straw-thin, matchstick-like chips.

Pommes rissolées Small round potatoes, deep-fried.

Pommes à la sarladaise Cubed potatoes sautéed in goose fat with truffles or wild mushrooms.

It is rectangular in shape and has a relatively mild taste.

Porc

Pork. A cornerstone of French cuisine, pork appears in a huge range of dishes and, of course, in the *charcuterie*, where, it is claimed, every part of the pig is used except for the squeak. *Fromage de porc* is a rather confusing name, which means brawn, not cheese.

Porché

Stewed pigs' ears and feet, from Brittany.

Port-Salut

A mild cows' milk cheese from Brittany, very similar to St-Paulin in taste.

Pot, au

Cooked in a pot, usually meaning boiled.

Potage

Soup. In general, it is lighter than its counterpart, *soupe*.

Potage bonne femme

A leek and potato soup not unlike *vichyssoise*.

Potage Crécy

Carrot soup.

Potage parmentier
A potato-based soup, usually with leeks added.

Potage paysanne
A straightforward soup made from mixed vegetables.

Pot-au-feu
A traditional French dish, a hearty mix of boiled beef, usually with carrots, leeks, turnips and potatoes. Originally from the southwest of France, it is now likely to be found everywhere. There are even *pot-au-feu* stock cubes available to buy.

Potée
A thick soup of bacon, cabbage and potatoes.

Potiron
Pumpkin. Used often in France for soups.

Poulet, poularde, poulette
Various names for chicken.

Poulet à l'estragon
Chicken with tarragon (see recipe, pages 142–3).

Poulet au vinaigre
Chicken cooked with shallots, wine vinegar and cream. From the Lyonnais, this is a very tasty dish. (Vinegar is quite often used in French cooking instead of wine.)

Poulet Marengo
A dish of chicken cooked with garlic, mushrooms and tomatoes.

Poulpe
Octopus. *Poulpe frit*, fried and crisp; otherwise stewed, perhaps *à la provençale* with onions, garlic and tomatoes.

Some French dishes make a tasty feature of octopus – poulpe.

Pourly
Small cylindrical goats' milk cheese from Burgundy.

Poussin
Baby chicken.

Praire
Clam.

Praliné(e)
Caramelised or covered with crushed toffee.

Presskopf
Type of brawn from Alsace.

Printanière, à la
Referring to spring. A dish, often lamb, accompanied by young mixed vegetables tossed in butter.

Profiteroles
Choux pastry buns filled with cream, sometimes topped with chocolate sauce.

Provençal
Meaning cooked the traditional Provençal way, usually with olive oil, tomatoes, peppers, garlic and anchovies.

Prune
Plum, not prune.

Pruneau
Prune.

Q

Quenelle
Oval mousse of puréed fish or white meat poached in liquid; for example, *quenelles de brochet* (pike). *Quenelles* are found in restaurants all over France. They are shaped using two spoons and poached to turn out rather like very light dumplings. However the same mixture may be set in a mould to cook in a *bain marie* (a container of water).

Quercy, Bleu du
A blue-veined cheese from the area around Figeac. It tastes very much like the better-known Bleu d'Auvergne.

Quetsch
Plum. Plums are also called *prunes*, while the prune itself is a *pruneau*.

Queue de boeuf
Oxtail.

Quiche
Savoury egg custard-filled pastry flan. There are many varieties of quiche. Miniature versions are often served as an *amuse-gueule* – an appetiser before a meal in many good restaurants.

Quiche Lorraine
The classic quiche, with diced bacon and cream, which comes from Lorraine.

R

Rabot
Whole apple cooked in pastry. A popular dessert from Champagne.

Racine
Root vegetable – turnip, carrot, and so on. The word *racine* means root.

Raclette

A traditional Savoie dish of melted cheese scraped (*racler*) over potatoes and cured meats. A ski resort favourite.

Radis

Radish.

Ragoût

A stew, usually a hearty version, prepared peasant-style.

Raie

Ray or skate. Often served simply, cooked in butter.

Raifort

Horseradish.

Raisin

Grape. The word *grappe*, which people sometimes use by mistake, means a bunch of something, not necessarily grapes.

Ramequin

A small individual pot, used mainly for baking an egg, or egg and cheese dishes.

Ramereau or ramier

Woodpigeon.

Râpé

Grated. In the supermarkets you will often find packs of ready-grated cheese, such as Gruyère, and grated carrot for salads.

Râpée

Thick grated potato pancake, similar to the Swiss *rösti*, which comes from the Lyonnais. The raw potato is first coarsely grated into a pan of foaming butter and oil, then is cooked on one side, before being turned over.

Ratatouille

Provençal dish of aubergines (eggplants), peppers, tomatoes, courgettes and garlic, cooked in olive oil. It is usually served as a side dish, but it also makes a good lunch dish if you are self-catering. *Ratatouille* is delicious served either hot or cold, along with chunks of French bread (see recipe, page 137).

Rave

Turnip.

Ravigote, sauce

Piquant *vinaigrette* with capers and chopped gherkins.

Reblochon

A delicious AOC cheese from Savoie. It is made from cows' milk and has a creamy taste. It is used as a topping for the alpine dish *tartiflette*.

Réchauffé

Reheated, made with cooked meat.

Reine, à la

With chicken.

Reine-Claude

Greengage. A very popular fruit in France, grown widely in the Dordogne.

Rémoulade

Mayonnaise seasoned with mustard and herbs, capers or gherkins. Often served spooned over shredded celeriac.

The famous French quiche, here seen beautifully presented.

Riceys, les

A cows' milk cheese that comes from the Troyes area, south of Champagne. It has a soft texture and comes in flat discs covered in wood ash.

Rigotte

A typical cylindrical goats' milk cheese from Ardèche, sold under the name of Rigotte de Condrieu or Rigotte de Pelusin.

Rillettes

Pork, occasionally goose or even rabbit, that is slow-cooked for a long time in its own fat, before being shredded and potted. It is then usually served spread on bread. It is not as savoury as pâté but very similar in appearance. You will find them on the menu all over central France.

Rillons

Crisp pieces of cooked pork or goose, which are browned and preserved in fat. The name is probably a contraction of *grillon*. *Rillons* have a very different texture to *rillettes*, with which they are often confused. A speciality of Touraine.

Ris

Veal or lamb sweetbreads. Many people misread the menu and order these by mistake, thinking that they have ordered rice (*riz*) instead.

Rissole

Deep-fried fritter, like a meatball. It can occasionally turn out to be a ball of vegetables or fish.

Rissolé

Baked brown, fried.

Riz

Rice. *Riz au blanc* is plain white boiled rice, while *riz au gras* is fried rice.

Rogeret de Cévennes

A goats' milk cheese with a colourful rind. It is very similar to Pélardon, which is from the same area.

Rognon

Kidney. Used in a number of French dishes.

Rognons Turbigo

A popular kidney dish with sausages, mushrooms, white wine and tomato sauce.

Romarin

Rosemary.

Rond de gigot

Thick slice of leg of mutton.

Roquefort

Probably the most popular blue-veined cheese in France, with an AOC rating. It is made from ewes' milk in Cévennes. Roquefort is matured for three months or more in the caves of Roquefort-sur-Soulzon before being sold. It has a very salty taste and a crumbly texture.

Rosbif

Roast beef. In France if you see this on the menu, it is usually served very rare, sliced and cold, possibly as part of an *assiette anglaise* – meaning a plate of cold cooked meats.

Rôti

Roasted.

Rouget

Red mullet.

Rouille

A hot, garlicky sauce in which soaked bread is mixed with garlic and paprika or cayenne pepper, or sometimes with canned sweet red pepper. This is an essential accompaniment, served spread on slices of French bread, to fish soups in Provence (see recipe, pages 133–4).

Roulade

Rolled and stuffed. The term usually refers to meat, but is sometimes used for fish or an omelette.

Roulé

Sweet or savoury roll.

Roussette

Dogfish.

Rouy

A soft cheese made from cows' milk that is manufactured in Dijon and sold in square boxes. It has a powerful smell.

Ruffec

A disc-shaped cheese from Charente. It is made from goats' milk, as most cheeses from this area are, but it has a fuller taste than most of the other varieties.

Rutabaga

Swede.

S

Sabayon
Dessert made from egg yolks, sugar and wine. Similar to Italian *zabaione* and sometimes served as a sauce.

Saignant
Meaning 'bleeding', this is a very rare steak.

St-Benoît, St-Benoist
A round fruity cheese from the Loire, made from cows' milk.

St-Florentin
Another round cheese, this time from Burgundy. It is made from cows' milk, and has a distinctive brownish-red rind and a full taste.

Ste-Foy, Bleu de Ste-Foy
A blue-veined cheese from cows' milk. It has a strong taste.

St-Gildas-des-Bois
A rich triple-cream cheese from Brittany, made with cows' milk. It has a rather mouldy smell.

St-Honoré
Gâteau of choux pastry and confectioner's custard.

St-Jacques
Abbreviation of *coquille St-Jacques*; scallop.

St-Marcellin, Tomme de St-Marcellin
A mild cows' cheese from Savoie.

Ste-Maure
A strong-smelling and -tasting goats' milk cheese from the Loire.

It is cylindrical and has a distinctive stick of straw running through the centre.

St-Nectaire
Hardish cheese from the Massif Central, made from cows' milk and sold in large wheels. It has an AOC rating, and smells rather mildewy – not surprisingly since it is usually ripened in local caves.

St-Paulin
A round cheese with a distinctive orange rind, made from cows' milk all over the north of France. It is fairly hard and mild, and tastes like Port-Salut.

St-Pierre
John Dory (fish).

St-Rémy
A strong-smelling cheese from Lorraine with a spicy taste. It is made from cows' milk, has a reddish rind and a square shape.

Salade
Salad (see box, page 78).

Salaison
Salted meat or fish *hors d'oeuvres* with anchovies, olives, etc.

Salé
Salted.

Salicorne
Samphire. See *passe-pierre*.

Salmis
Game casserole, where the meat is first roasted then finished in wine sauce; rather similar to braised dishes.

Salpicon

An old French word for fish or meat with diced vegetables in one of a variety of sauces or, if cold, with a mayonnaise. The result is used as a rather rarified stuffing. Often used to fill little pastry *barquettes* served as appetisers or *hors d'oeuvres*.

Salsifis

Salsify, the oyster plant. It is either served young, eaten raw in a salad or cooked with a *béchamel* sauce. *Scorzonera* is a root vegetable closely related to salsify. Salsify is a white root, while *scorzonera* is black-skinned.

Sandwich

Roll or piece of long loaf, often filled with ham. A French sandwich made with a split *ficelle* or a *baguette*, stuffed full of pâté and salad, makes a meal in itself. A more elegant version can be made by using a *brioche* filled with *pâté de foie gras* – easier on the teeth too.

Sanglier

Wild boar. It has a gamey taste that does not bear much resemblance to ordinary pork. You will find that wild boar features quite frequently on the menu in the countryside. Wild boar pâté is considered to be a delicacy. You can find it on sale in mountainous places as far south as Sault in Provence. However, its taste can be a little disappointing, and it may be expensive, so try it before you buy a jar or two to take home.

SIMPLE OR SOPHISTICATED SALADS

The most simple, classic French salad consists of only fresh, perfect lettuce, torn by hand and served with an oil and vinegar dressing. A *salade simple* is a plain salad. A *salade composée* is a substantial mixed salad with eggs, beans, ie something fairly hearty, in it. *Salade panachée* is an ordinary mixed salad. A green salad is a *salade verte*. You may be asked if you want it *avec* or *sans l'ail* – with or without garlic. *Salade de fruits* is fruit salad.

Salade niçoise Salad from Nice, of tomatoes, peppers, French beans, olives, anchovies and eggs. It varies in size, depending on whether it is served as a starter or a main dish. Tuna is often added for a more substantial salad (see recipe, pages 134–135).

Salade Russe Russian salad of diced root vegetables in mayonnaise.

Saladier Large mixed bowl of salad.

A FOOD OF MANY FORMS

France has a huge variety of sausages ranging from the fiery *merguez*, which has to be cooked, to *saucisse à l'ail* (garlic sausage). Air-dried sausages, sometimes called *saucisson de montagne*, are eaten raw, others need poaching or frying first. Use your common sense when buying. On the whole, the large sausages (*saucissons*) are pre-cooked, ready to slice and eat, the small ones (*saucisses*) will need cooking. If you object to eating horse, avoid any sausage that has the word *cheval* attached to it. French *charcutiers* must, by law, declare the contents of sausages made from mule, horse or donkey.

Sassenage
A blue-veined cheese from Savoie, usually made from a mix of cows' and goats' milk.

Saucisse, saucisson
Types of sausage (see box, above).

Saumon
Salmon. A fish that is enjoyed as much in France as anywhere else, including *saumon fumé* (smoked salmon). *Darne de saumon* is a salmon steak.

Saumon blanc
Not salmon at all, but the humble hake (*colin*).

Saupiquet
In the Languedoc, roast hare in a spicy blood and onion sauce. Elsewhere the term may just denote a spicy wine and vinegar sauce.

Sauté
To cook quickly in shallow oil or fat over high heat.

Savarin
Classic light, sponge-like ring, often cooked in a decorative mould, made with yeast batter. It is covered with syrup and fruit, then drenched in rum or *kirsch*.

Savaron
A daunting-looking round cheese from Auvergne with a thick covering of mildew on the outside. Actually it has a mild taste, is semi-hard and is made from cows' milk.

Savoyarde, à la
Indicates the presence of potatoes and cheese.

Scarole
Curly-leaved Batavian endive. One of the slightly bitter ingredients that the sensible French include in their green salads. Delicious with dressing, it makes most lettuce seem bland and characterless.

Scorsonère, scorzonera
See *salsifis*.

Seiche

Cuttlefish. You will occasionally find this mixed in with seafood dishes. Basically rather tough to eat, cuttlefish is beaten before cooking, then sliced and cooked like octopus, with which you may confuse it.

Sel

Salt.

Selle

Saddle, referring to lamb, goat or venison.

Selles-sur-Cher

The name of a town in the Cher region and also a fine AOC goats' milk cheese, whose rind is dusted with black powdered charcoal. It also goes under the name of Romorantin, and has a delicate mild flavour.

Selon grosseur

Price according to size, for example, for lobster.

Septmoncel, Bleu de

A blue cheese from the Jura, made from cows' milk. It has a rather sharp taste and is very similar to Bleu de Gex, which is made nearby.

Sole

Sole. This fish is found extensively in northern France and is used for a number of classic dishes.

Sole bonne femme

Sole poached in white wine with mushrooms.

Sole Colbert

Sole coated in egg and breadcrumbs, then fried and served with *maître d'hôtel* (parsley and lemon juice) butter.

French sole features widely in the cooking of northern France.

Sole meunière
Sole fried with lemon and herbs.

Soubise
Onion and cream sauce, or one made with a purée of onions and rice. Usually served with meat.

Soumaintrain
A strong cheese from Burgundy, made with cows' milk. It has a slightly spicy flavour, and is round and flat with a washed orange rind.

Soupe
Soup. Although soup does not appear on the menu quite as frequently as it used to, you will still find it in country areas. The difference between *soupe* and *potage* is that the former tends to be on the hearty side – almost a meal in itself – whereas *potage* is usually of a less filling consistency.

Soupe à l'ail
Garlic soup. Usually found in the Basque region, anywhere in the direction of Spain.

Soupe à l'oignon
The famous French onion soup, served with grated cheese and chunky bread.

Soupe au pistou
From the south, a soup with a distinct flavour of basil as well as garlic, containing vegetables and *pistou* (like *pesto*; see recipe, pages 132–3).

Soupe de poisson
A smooth fish soup from the Mediterranean. Served with squares of toast, *rouille* and grated cheese. It differs from the well-known *bouillabaisse* in that there are not chunks of fish or bones in it, everything having been sieved (see recipe, pages 133–4).

Spécialité
Speciality.

Steak, bifteck
Beef steak. The four typical stages of cooking (*cuisson*) are: *bleu* (just sealed on the outside); *saignant* (very rare); *à point* (theoretically medium); *bien cuit* (well-done – but specify *très bien cuit* if you cannot bear a trace of pink).

Sucre
Sugar.

Suprème
Although the word sounds as though it is referring to the quality of the meat, it actually means breast of chicken, or occasionally of game bird.

T

Tamié
A cows' milk cheese made by the Trappist monks at the monastery of Tamié, near Lake Annecy. It is smooth and round, and sometimes goes under the name of *Trappiste de Tamié*.

Tapenade

A Provençal paste made from black olives and capers that are pounded with anchovies with a little olive oil and lemon. Tapenade is usually served in little pots as an appetiser, along with chunks of toasted French bread.

Tapéno

Caper. These seeds of a Mediterranean shrub look and taste very like nasturtium seeds, which are often used as a substitute.

Tartare

A sharp sauce made from mayonnaise with capers, gherkins and herbs, which is usually served with fish. It is also the brand name of a herb-flavoured cream cheese from Périgord.

Tartiflette

Cubed or sliced potatoes with bacon *lardons*, onions and *crème fraîche*, covered with disks of Reblochon cheese and baked. A winter dish from Savoie.

Tartine

Slice of bread and butter, sometimes jam. The name is also used for a small tart.

Tartine suisse

Puff pastry with vanilla cream.

Terrine

Form of potted meat or pâté. The main difference between a pâté and a terrine is that the latter is usually coarser.

Tête

Head, eg calf's head (*tête de veau*).

Tétras

Grouse.

Thiézac, Bleu de

A cheese very like Bleu d'Auvergne, which also comes from the Auvergne area. It is made from cows' milk.

Thon

Tuna fish.

Tian

Provençal word for food baked, sometimes grilled, in a shallow terracotta dish of the same name.

Tiède

Warm.

Tignes, Bleu de

Another of the family of blue cheeses from Savoie. It is small and round and made from cows' milk.

Tomme

There are literally hundreds of Tomme cheeses, all totally different. This is because the word refers to the container in which the cheeses, usually from mountainous areas, are made.

Tomme d'Annot

A cheese from the Haute-Alpes that may be made from goats' or ewes' milk.

Tomme de Cantal

A cheese from the Auvergne and usually made from cows' milk but sometimes from goats' milk. It is used a great deal in cooking.

Olives sold fresh and as tapenade, *for sale at a Paris market.*

Tomme de Savoie
A larger cheese from the Savoie mountains. It is made with cows' milk and has a fairly firm texture.

Tomme du Mont-Ventoux
A cheese from the mountain of that name that overlooks the Luberon valley in Provence. Made from ewes' milk, it is fresh and slightly salted.

Topinambour
Jerusalem artichoke.

Tournedos
Small beef fillet.

Tournedos Rossini
Steak with truffles, *foie gras* and Madeira sauce.

Tournon Saint-Pierre
A cone-shaped cheese from Poitou-Charentes. Made from cows' milk, it has a strong smell, although its texture is soft.

Touron
Nut-covered almond pastry from the South of France.

Tourte
Usually a savoury pie or covered tart. A *tarte*, on the other hand, is usually sweet.

Tranche
Slice, rasher. A *tranche* can also mean a chop, so do not be surprised if it has bones.

Tripe, oeufs à la
Nothing whatsoever to do with tripe but a name for chopped hard-boiled eggs with onions, from Normandy.

Tripe, tripailles
Tripe, ox stomach, a food that is still popular in France.

Tripes à la mode de Caen
Tripe stewed with onions and herbs in cider and/or Calvados; probably the classic tripe dish.

Troo

The name of the cheese from the village in the Loire valley where the late British cookery writer Jane Grigson lived. It is made from goats' milk and is mild and cone-shaped.

Truffado

A delicious savoury dish made from potatoes fried with bacon, garlic and cheese that comes from the Auvergne.

Truffe

Truffle. A revered and very expensive delicacy in France, truffles taste rather like highly perfumed, earthy mushrooms. Known as 'black gold', they are hunted out from the roots of truffle oak trees in the Dordogne and Provence by men with specially trained dogs – originally pigs were used. Truffles are used mainly for garnishes as their price generally precludes them from being the main feature of a meal. If you want to try truffles for yourself, a good way is to buy the smallest you can find, set it among a bowl of eggs so that the perfume permeates the shells, then use them to make delicious truffle omelettes. A real treat.

Truffé, trufflé, trufflée

Garnished or stuffed with truffles. The small square of dark brown decoration in the aspic on a cold dish will almost certainly be a piece of truffle.

Truite

Trout. *Truite arc-en-ciel* is rainbow trout, while *Truite de mer* refers to salmon trout.

Ttoro Basquaise

Stew of fish, tomatoes, onion and garlic.

V

Vachard

A strong cheese from the Massif Central, made from cows' milk. It is very similar to St-Nectaire.

Vacherin

Meringue filled with strawberries, ice-cream and whipped cream. It is also the name given to several superb cheeses made with cows' milk. These are usually soft and runny, and come from the Jura or the Savoie mountains. Vacherin Mont-d'Or is the best of them all, and is made only during winter.

Valençay

A goats' milk cheese hailing from the Loire. It is shaped like a truncated pyramid, and is coated in charcoal ashes.

Vapeur, au

Meaning steamed, the term is usually used to refer to potatoes.

Varié
Meaning assorted; *hors d'oeuvres variés*, for instance, indicates a plate of assorted types of *hors d'oeuvres*.

Veau
Veal; this meat is used throughout France, particularly in the north of the country. *Escalope de veau* refers to a flattened veal slice, which may be served in many different ways. A *paupiette de veau* is a slice of veal that comes rolled round a filling, often pâté or ham.

Veau, blanquette de
Breast of veal cooked in a white sauce.

Venaison
Venison. See *chevreuil*.

Vendômois
A farm cheese from Vendôme in the Loire. A young goats' milk cheese with a dusting of ash.

Vermicelle
Vermicelli.

Vert(e)
Green, as in *salade verte*.

Verte, sauce
Green herb mayonnaise.

Vézelay
A Burgundian cheese made from goats' milk. It comes in a conical shape and has a rather strong flavour.

Viande
Meat.

Vichyssoise
The famous, smooth and creamy leek and potato soup. It is usually served chilled but tastes equally good when eaten piping hot in winter.

Vigneron, à la
The term usually refers to meat that is served with a wine sauce of some kind, and garnished with grapes.

Vinaigre
Vinegar. Plain vinegar in France is wine vinegar (*vinaigre de vin*), which is less acrid than malt vinegar. The French have an enormous range of flavoured vinegars, most of them red or white wine-based. The best known are tarragon vinegar (*vinaigre à l'estragon*) and shallot vinegar (*vinaigre à l'echalote*), which is one of the traditional accompaniments to oysters.

Vinaigrette, sauce
The classic French salad dressing, made with a base of vinegar and oil. To give it their own personal signature, each cook adds something extra: a spot of sugar, perhaps, some mustard or garlic.

Volaille
Poultry.

Vol-au-vent
Puff pastry case filled with meat or fish.

W

Y

Waterzooï
From Flanders, this stew either comes *de poisson*, which contains freshwater fish and herbs, or *de volaille*, indicating that it is made from chicken with leeks and cream.

Williams
A type of pear. A pear is quite often referred to simply as Williams without the addition of the word '*poire*'.

Witloof
Chicory.

Yaourt
Yoghurt. This now comes in every conceivable flavouring in the supermarkets, with full-fat and low-fat versions both available to buy.

Chicory, with its slightly bitter taste, makes an interesting addition to many French dishes.

Wine and Drink of France

Lush vineyards of the Rhône, overlooked by a small hillside village.

These black grapes are ripe and ready to harvest.

Wine and Drink of France

France – home to the famous
Bordeaux, Burgundy and Champagne
areas, to name just three – is indis-
putably the greatest wine-producing
country in the world, and the French
are justly proud of their reputation and
long wine-producing history. You will
find a vast variety of whites, reds and
rosés on offer, from the best-quality
vintages down to the humble *vin de
pays* (the local wines). But although
French wines are all basically made the

same way, how they turn out depends, to a large extent, on a complex
balance of soil type, climate, the choice and colour of the grape and how
long they are allowed to remain in the fermenting vats. That being so, rosé
wines do not keep very well, white wines (with certain notable exceptions) have a relatively short life, and it is the heavier reds that are
bought to lay down for years to come. Champagnes may be matured for
many years, but only while they are in the producers' *caves*. Once the
bottle is finally corked and put on sale it will not go on to improve greatly if
allowed to age further.

As an alternative to wine, the ciders of Brittany and Normandy taste
quite unlike some of the mass-produced ciders you may have encoun-
tered, being thirst-quenching and full of character. But be careful not
to underestimate their potency. Calvados, the famous apple brandy, is
often made in small copper stills on farms in the valley of the Auge, in
Normandy. If you are touring, it pays to visit the farms in the Calvados
area and buy direct.

Alsace-Lorraine has several spas and from here come many fine mineral
waters, Vittel and Contrexéville being the most famous. This region also
produces a great deal of beer from the hops grown nearby. The Loire
valley has contributed perhaps one of the best-known drinks in France,
Cointreau, the orange-flavoured liqueur.

Wine-Producing Regions

The largest wine-producing areas are located in the centre of France – Bordeaux and Burgundy (Bourgogne), both of which are on roughly the same parallel – while the best known of all must be Champagne, farther north. Unfortified wines basically fall into two categories, still or sparkling, but there is a third type that you will come across, particularly in places such as Vouvray, and that is *pétillant* – a wine with a slight natural bubble in it that just prickles on the tongue and no more.

Apart from the extreme north, where beers and ciders hold sway, all districts of France produce a local wine of some sort. Wherever you stay, you are bound to find something you like from this huge variety to accompany a meal, whether it is one of the flowery German-style Rieslings of Alsace, the light rosés from Provence that give an immediate touch of summer sun, the light-hearted Beaujolais wines or the important and heavier clarets from Bordeaux.

CHAMPAGNE

There may be many good sparkling wines in the world but there is, quite simply, no substitute for champagne. And the reason is not just the chalky slopes on which the grapes are grown, but the immense trouble and attention to detail that goes into making this great celebratory drink. It has a freshness that no other white wine – even the splendid sparkling wines of the Loire – can quite attain.

Sparkling wine is made in several different ways. At the very cheapest end of the market, gas from carbonic acid is simply injected in the wine. Then there is the *cuvée close* method, where it is re-fermented in large vats. But in the *méthode champenoise* the newly made still wine is re-fermented the following spring in individual bottles and gradually tipped and turned, over a period, so that sediment collects at the neck from where it is ejected. The wine is then dosed with a little sugar and given the famous wired cork. All this takes a long time, and vintage champagnes are not put on sale for years.

The cellars of the famous Mercier champagne house.

The wine is usually made from a mix of white Chardonnay and black Pinot Noir and Pinot Meunier grapes. The proportion varies from producer to producer, and influences the flavour and character of the wine. Champagne made exclusively from Chardonnay grapes will be labelled *Blanc de blancs*, while that made only from the Pinot grapes will have *Blanc de noirs* on the label.

In the case of pink champagne, the skins of the black grapes are allowed to stay a little longer in the fermented 'must' so that they colour it. Pink champagne is more popular in the rest of the world than it is in Champagne itself.

If you go to Épernay, at the Avenue de Champagne you will find the cellars of most of the famous makers. The majority of these run regular tours round their cellars, which are cut into solid chalk. Although they are run rather on a production-line basis – in one case you are taken round in something like the ghost train on a fairground – you do get your chance to sip the product at the end.

Vintage champagne (ie, wine with a year stated on the label) is produced only in truly exceptional years. Currently, 2002 is a year to look out for.

BORDEAUX

This is almost undoubtedly the greatest wine-making area in France and the place where some of the most famous names come from. Wines from this area have long been popular with the British, and Bordeaux's Atlantic position has also led to a strong US connection.

This area produces more wine in volume than any other part of France. So it is difficult to know where to begin when talking about Bordeaux wines, for there are more fine vintages encompassed here than anywhere else in the world, especially from the Médoc to the north. There are the St-Émilions, the Pomerols, those from Château Lafite, Margaux and Pauillac, for instance. Bordeaux wines are so important that they are divided into *Crus*. The term takes on a special meaning for Bordeaux wines and indicates that they are of a superior quality or from a château of repute, not simply from a particular area.

Bordeaux wines, most of them red, are inclined to be heavy and rather dry. Unlike wines from Burgundy, which can be drunk quite young, they should be allowed to age a little, if possible, or the taste of tannin may make your pallet curl. A cheap Bordeaux wine should be treated kindly – open it at least two hours before serving, decant it if possible. Or save up and buy a *Grand Cru* from St-Émilion. Made mainly from the Merlot grape, it is less harsh than some of the other clarets when young, and is a good buy. If you are likely to be impatient, choose a Pomerol, which matures

Bottles of Bordeaux's world-famous Château Margaux roll off the production line.

relatively fast. This complexity has caused something of a crisis in Bordeaux in recent years, as wine drinkers turned to more accessible and 'reliable' reds from more modern French producers and the New World. Belatedly, Bordeaux has looked to its laurels; it is revitalising production, quality and labelling, and has even introduced a new denomination, *vin de pays d'Atlantique*, for drinkable wines that do not merit the Bordeaux appellation.

The red wines of Bordeaux are traditionally known in Britain and the US as clarets, although the word is now sometimes used for wines from Australia and South America too. Although Bordeaux produces three bottles of red wine to every one of white, there are a number of interesting options in the latter category. White wines of note from this area include the sweetest wine of them all, Sauternes, which goes so well with puddings. It is made from grapes that have been left on the vine so long that they have begun to shrivel. Other white wines include the drier Entre-Deux-Mers, which comes from an area between the two rivers, the Dordogne and Garonne. Graves is an interesting wine to try: the white is relatively dry, but there is a lesser-known red Graves that is a good light lunch drink. As for many French wines, 2005 was an excellent year, and Bordeaux's great wines of this vintage will continue to improve for up to 15 years.

BURGUNDY

Burgundy may not produce as large a quantity of wine as Bordeaux, but some of the best wines in the world come from its vineyards. These run in a strip along the main highway from Paris to the Mediterranean, south of Dijon. White wines such as Montrachet, Meursault, Chassagne-Montrachet and Corton-Charlemagne from the Côte de Beaune are produced here. On the red front the finest burgundies come from the vineyards of the Côte d'Or, which is sub-divided into the Côte de Nuits – famous for its Nuits-St-Georges and Gevrey-Chambertin – and the Côte de Beaune, the country seat of the Dukes of Burgundy, where Pommard, Volnay and Beaune itself are made. Further down comes the Mâcon district that produces both red and some very good white wines, including Pouilly-Fuissé, while among the top-quality but slightly cheaper reds worth trying is the full-bodied Mercurey. Sparkling wines are found in Rully, in the Chalon area, made properly by the *méthode champenoise*. For the world-famous Chablis you must make a detour and venture northwest of Dijon, to a tiny outpost of Burgundy in the Yonne. The weather and soil here give the wine a different character from the buttery notes found in the Côte d'Or, despite it being made from the same Chardonnay grape. Chablis is prized for its lemony, steel and mineral notes.

However, big business though they may be, these wines are of less interest to the ordinary visitor to France than those of the delightful Beaujolais district around Villefranche-sur-Saône in the south, with its more informal fruity reds. Here, among the gentle hills, are a series of villages such as Brouilly, Fleurie, Juliénas, each producing its own special wine in an atmosphere that is more relaxed, and less commercial. (Vaux en Beaujolais, by the way, is the origin of Clochemerle, the town in the satirical novel of the same name by Gabriel Chavallier, and there is a 'Cave de Clochemerle' in a neighbouring village, Ste-Lager, where the film of the book was made.)

Beaujolais comes in four ranks: simple Beaujolais, which is the cheapest; *Beaujolais supérieur*, which costs a little more; then *Beaujolais Villages*; and, finally, the wines named after the vineyards – Chiroubles, Morgon, Chénas, Moulin-à-Vent and so on. Of all the *routes du vin* (the vineyard drives), the one through the Beaujolais region is perhaps the most rewarding and charming. There is none of the grandeur of, say, Mâcon or Beaune, because wine-making here seems to be more of a cottage industry. So make a point, if you can, of visiting these places and trying their wines.

Like Bordeaux, Burgundy's 2005 vintage is the one to seek out, for both red and white wines.

THE LOIRE

Some of the freshest, most delightful white wines of France come from this area. Muscadet is produced around Nantes at the mouth of the River Loire. It is very dry and ideal with seafood, and is found in abundance in local restaurants.

If you like your white wine less crisp, then try Sancerre or Pouilly-Fumé, both of which hail from the Loire valley and both of which are made from the Sauvignon Blanc grape. The grape's nettle and gooseberry flavours also perfume the increasingly popular white wines of the Touraine. The red wines of the Loire, on the other hand, from Chinon, Saumur and

Bourgueil, are lighter and softer to the taste than those of neighbouring Bordeaux, and they make a particularly good choice for lunchtime drinking. Saumur also produces a sparkling white wine that is fermented in the bottle by the *méthode champenoise*. Then there are the great white wines of Vouvray to consider, made from the Chenin Blanc grape, sold sparkling, still or *pétillant*. A dry sparkling Vouvray, well-chilled, can almost masquerade as champagne. If you missed out on a wine tour in champagne country, it is well worth touring the caves of Vouvray to see how they do it.

Anjou is known for its rather unremarkable rosé wine, but it is also home to some superb sweet wines, such as Bonnezeaux. Again, 2005 was a classic year.

ALSACE

If you like the fruity flavour of German white wine, then this is the place for you. For not only are the vineyards near the German border, but the same grape varieties are grown: Gewurztraminer, Riesling, Sylvaner to name just a few. They go perfectly with the rich rather heavy food served in the area, and even if you are not normally a fan of this strong, flowery taste, you are likely to be converted when you sample them *in situ*.

Almost all wines from Alsace and Lorraine are white, but if you are visiting the area you will come across a local red that looks washed out in colour compared with one, say, from Burgundy. There is also *vin gris*, a very pale rosé, which you may be offered in local restaurants.

The wines are named by the grapes (*cépages*) – Riesling, for instance – rather than by the vineyards, which tend to remain relatively anonymous. The lightest wines are those made from the Chasselas grape. The four *Grand Cru* varieties are Riesling, Gerwurztraminer, Muscat and Pinot Gris. If you see the word *Edelzwicker* on a label, this indicates that the wine is made not from a single grape variety but from a blend of several. If you ask for a local wine in most cafés in Alsace, that is what you are likely to be served, usually in rather squat glasses with thick green stems.

The wines to drink before dinner, or on a summer night, are the Sylvaners. Leave the Rieslings for the main course of the meal. If you like sparkling wines, Alsace has its own local version, *Crémant d'Alsace*, which is fermented in the bottle like champagne. Alsace is also the place to sample a whole host of spirits based on fruits, called *eaux-de-vie*.

The village of Eze in Provence has a stunning location overlooking the Mediterranean Sea.

THE SOUTH

Although only a few really stunning wines come from the South of France, there are some interesting examples to be found, grown in such diverse conditions as the sand of the Camargue – which produces the famous Listel branded range of wines – to the rocky soil of Corbières near Narbonne, or the stone-littered vineyards of the Rhône valley. The northern Rhône makes some hearty reds such as Côte-Rôtie and Hermitage, featuring the Syrah grape (the Shiraz of New World wines), and offering smoky berry and chocolate notes. Whites such as Condrieu feature the rising-star grape Viognier, with its apricot and honey flavours.

To go with the long hot Provençal summers come a whole host of rosés that never taste quite the same, somehow, when you get them back home. Equally good drunk straight, iced or laced with sparkling mineral water, rosé, like *pastis* (aniseed-based drinks), is the drink of the south. The cheaper rosés are often high in alcohol and low in finesse, and a day spent supping in the sun can end in headaches.

However, a great many lighter, more elegant wines, are now being made. The most famous option is Tavel, but there are a whole host of others such as Côtes du Luberon and Côtes de Ventoux, which is named after the mountain of that name. Being so far south, production at this level tends to be of red or rosé rather than white wines. The white wine called Cassis has nothing to do with the blackcurrant liqueur, but is named after the small coastal resort of that name near Marseille. The southern Rhône gives Provence its most popular red wines, such as Châteauneuf-du-Pape and Côtes-du-Rhône-Villages, but perhaps the best comes from Bandol, where the Mourvèdre grape gives a velvety texture after ageing.

The vineyards of the Languedoc-Roussillon region have experienced a revolution in recent years. Once famous mainly for turning out wine lakes of indifferent Vin de Pays d'Oc, now acres of vineyards have been dug up and what remains is in the hands of dynamic young *vignerons* who have learned great lessons from New World wine-makers. The white wines come from the area around Narbonne, near the coast, and there is a sparkling white wine from Limoux that is made by the champagne method and, therefore, keeps its bubbles.

Apart from Corbières, another good red wine worth trying comes from the Minervois.

A Selection of Wines

The wines shown here are just a personal selection from the vast variety – over 700 at the last count – to be found in France. The grape varieties used in the making of the wines are shown. There is a reason for this: having found a grape variety whose taste appeals to you – the rich blackberry-like Cabernet Sauvignon, for instance, or the flowery, fruity Germanic tones of a Sylvaner or Riesling – it is on the cards that if you are choosing blind, another wine made from the same grape will suit.

If you are travelling it always pays to ask for a local wine in restaurants. Not only will you earn the proprietor's approval, but it will normally be served with great pride, and you will be told all about the wine.

Beaujolais

Made from the Gamay grape, this jolly, red AC wine is lighter than those from Bordeaux. It can tend to be rather uninteresting, so it is worth paying a little extra for a Beaujolais-Villages, one step up in quality. Better still are the ten named village wines, including Juliénas, Moulin-à-Vent, Fleurie or Brouilly, probably the best of them all. The trend has finally moved away from Beaujolais Nouveau, but it can still be a pleasant treat to sample it on release in late November, with its vibrant purple hue and almost banana-ish flavour.

Chablis

A white AC burgundy (the wine actually has a greenish tinge) made from the Chardonnay grape. It goes well with shellfish and *hors d'oeuvres*, and comes in three qualities: *Grand Cru, Premier Cru* and *Petit Chablis,* the last of which should be drunk within three years.

Champagne

The world's most famous wine that must, by law, come only from the vineyards of the Champagne district around Reims. Vintage champagne can cost an amazing amount of money, but non-vintage varieties can still be found at reasonable prices. You will be surprised to find, however, that you have to pay almost as much for it in France as in Britain. It is made from the Chardonnay, Pinot Noir and Pinot Meunier grape varieties.

Château Mouton-Rothschild

One of the most famous wines in the world, which, along with Château Lafite and Château Latour, all come from the village of Pauillac in the Médoc. Expect to pay a great deal of money for these wines, but to drink one is an unforgettable experience – especially if you can persuade someone else to foot the bill.

Châteauneuf-du-Pape

The best-known classic AC Rhône red with a purple tinge and high alcohol content. This is made from a blend of over a dozen different grapes, including the strong Syrah, Grenache and Mourvèdre. The vineyard was set up for the popes when they ruled from Avignon in the 14th century. It was under Pope John XXII, who built the iconic castle (the Château Neuf) here, that the wines became known as *vin du Pape* ('the Pope's wine') before taking on the name it bears today. These wines need strongly flavoured food to go with them.

Côtes du Rhône

A robust red, with a high alcohol content – at least 12 degrees – from the Rhône valley. It is made from a mix of grapes, almost always including Syrah. Quality varies tremendously, but if you open the bottle and allow the wine to breathe for a couple of hours before serving it (better still, decant it first), it seems to take away the rough edge. This is a good everyday red to drink with strongly flavoured dishes including pasta. Try Gigondas, Lirac, Cairanne or Vacqueyras.

Entre-Deux-Mers

A fresh and fruity dry white AC wine from between the rivers Garonne and Dordogne (the two 'seas' in the name) in Bordeaux. Sauvignon Blanc gives the wine its aromatic appeal.

Fitou

These AC red wines come from the Corbières region of Languedoc-Roussillon. Those from near the coast (Fitou Maritime) are light and may be drunk young, while the inland wines (Fitou Montagneux) improve with age.

Graves

Another classic Bordeaux AC white wine. Sometimes sweet but more usually dry, made from Sauvignon Blanc and Sémillon grapes. There are also red Graves that are rather more interesting. The expensive and elegant Château Haut-Brion is one such.

Hermitage

Deep, dark reds from the northern Rhône that benefit from years of maturity to reach their peak.

Médoc

The generic name given to a range of AC wines coming from the area of that name in Bordeaux and including very expensive, great wines such as Château Margaux. A wine simply labelled Médoc is usually a better choice with your meal than one called claret or any other ordinary Bordeaux. Wines labelled AC Haut-Médoc are of slightly better quality and, therefore, more expensive.

Mercurey

This wine from Burgundy's Côte Chalonnaise is expensive, but it has a splendid, classy flavour and matures quicker than many others from the same area. Like many Burgundy wines, it is often labelled under the name of a *négociant*, or shipper. A reliable name to look out for is Bouchard-Aîné.

Meursault

An outstanding white burgundy from the Montrachet area; golden and buttery, it is still drier and less heavy than other Montrachet wines and goes well with fish.

Montrachet

One of several famous AC white wines, some of them *Grand Cru*, from the Burgundy area. Look out for Puligny-Montrachet and Chassagne-Montrachet.

Muscadet

A dry white wine from the Loire made from a grape of that name, which at its best is crisp and delicious, at its worst sharp and vinegary. It goes well with all kinds of fish, especially shellfish. Muscadet de Sèvre et Maine, an AOC wine, is a safe choice, with Muscadet des Coteaux de la Loire a close second. Muscadet *sur lie* is wine that has been bottled while it is on its lees (still fermenting), giving it a slight 'prickle' on the tongue. This phrase is worth looking out for on a label.

Nuits-St-Georges

A famous AC red burgundy. It comes from the Côte de Nuits, and is well worth drinking, if slightly expensive.

Pommard

A generic name for a group of fruity AC reds from Burgundy in the Côte de Beaune area. Individual names to look for on the label include Clos Micot and Clos des Épeneaux and the prestigious Les Rugiens.

Pouilly-Fuissé

A golden AC wine from the Mâconnais in Burgundy, best drunk young. It goes well with white meat, fish or *hors d'oeuvres*.

Pouilly-Fumé

Made from the Sauvignon Blanc grape, this is a slightly heavier AC white than Sancerre, its near neighbour. It cuts through rich sauces, goes well with fish and has an elegant finish, with a smoky (*fumé*) note.

Romanée-Conti

One of the smallest and most exclusive vineyards in the world – it covers only 1.8 hectares (4½ acres) – which produces a *Grand Cru* red burgundy that rates as one of the top international wines.

Sancerre

Crisp white AC wine from the Loire valley made from Sauvignon Blanc. It goes well with fish, of course, but is also good with white meat. If you want to progress in quality from Muscadet, this is a good wine to try.

Sauternes

A sweet white AC wine from southern Bordeaux made mainly from the Sémillon grape that is allowed to stay late on the vine to develop more sugar. It makes a wonderful partner to puddings.

Tavel

Argued by many to be the best rosé in France, made from Grenache and Cinsault grapes in vineyards in the Rhône valley. Do not drink it too cold or you will miss its elegant flavour. A spicy note makes it good to drink with Asian dishes.

Volnay

A light AC red burgundy that can be drunk very young. The vineyards are situated between Pommard and Meursault, and white wines grown in Volnay are sold as Meursault.

Touraine

The white Sauvignon Blanc wines of this region of the Loire are increasingly good and popular for their grassy, gooseberry flavours.

Vouvray

Delicious white AC wine, well worth keeping, that comes from the vineyards of the Loire valley. It is made from the Chenin Blanc grape, and the bottles are stored in limestone caves – worth a visit if you are in the area. Some types of Vouvray are slightly *pétillant*. Vouvray made in the *méthode champenoise* is a relatively inexpensive festive drink.

Wine Facts

Finding and enjoying good wines is a fun part of any holiday. It is a shame simply to rely on the restaurant or the supermarket for bottles, though. It is much better to be adventurous, taste some for yourself, then make up your own mind.

On the Label

All French wines are named either after the grape from which they are made – Chardonnay, for instance – or, more usually, after the place where the wine was made. It comes as a surprise, sometimes, to find that the big-name, expensive wine that you enjoy does not come from a superb château, set in rolling hectares of vines, but from a *négociant,* a big wine shipper, such as Sichel, with sober city premises.

There are, of course, plenty of wines that are *mis en bouteille* (bottled) on the premises, at the vineyard of origin or the place where the wine was produced – be it a château or a humble *cave* – but many more come from grapes collected from a variety of growers and blended in warehouse premises (a *Cave Co-opérative*).

The word *domaine*, which is sometimes seen on the label, also

APPELLATION D'ORIGINE

French wines are strictly controlled. The *Appellation d'Origine* system was set up and is still governed by the Institut National des Appellations d'Origine, which oversees the production of wine. Four categories are used for the *Appellation d'Origine* classification. The highest-ranking wines are the AOC wines that have an *Appellation Contrôlée*. These must come from a certain specified area and match a certain standard. They are strictly controlled in terms of the grapes, the growing of the vines and the production of the wine. Next down the quality list come the VDQS wines (*Vin Délimité de Qualité Supérieure*). These are superior regional wines. Then the *Vins de Pays* are good honest local wines. Finally there is *Vin de Table*, which is the equivalent of 'plonk', but can still be very good.

Sampling the wine is a must before buying – as at this wine fair in Vouvray.

sounds like a fine country house but is probably a large vineyard or just a company. And the fine oak casks are a thing of the past in many instances, having been replaced by more hygienic high-tech tanks of fibreglass or steel. The label will often say *Elevé en Fûts de Chêne* if the wine has been matured in oak.

Wine Tasting

Ask if it's possible to have a tasting – not from one of the grand châteaux (for that you would need to get an introduction from your local wine merchant back home first) – but from the ordinary producers.

The smaller the vineyard, the more likely you are to be invited in and made welcome. The word to look out for is *dégustation* (which means 'wine tasting') – you will see signs up on the road.

This is not a swirl in the glass, sniff and spit into a spittoon session, the kind of thing that Masters of Wine indulge in, but a no-nonsense sampling of the wine to see, quite simply, whether you like it or not before committing yourself to buying a bottle. Of course, they hope you will buy but no one will complain if you taste and then go away without purchasing anything (though, in some places, you may be charged

Grapes crated up and waiting to be transformed into wine.

a nominal amount per glass for the wine you consume).

Even the *Caves Co-opératives* have a tasting bar where you can sample their wares, and it often doubles as the local 'pub'. If you are ordering wine in a restaurant, the waiter will be delighted if you ask for a *vin de la région*, for they are bound to be proud of their own local wine.

Quaffing Wines

Ordinaires refer to ordinary wines from places such as Roussillon in the foothills of the Pyrenees. You will find these served all over France, and all are perfectly drinkable and cheap.

If you want to quaff wine rather than sip it appreciatively, and are therefore buying in bulk, in country areas you will find *Caves Co-opératives* or look out for the sign *Depot de Vente*, where *ordinaires* are served up like petrol. It is a fascinating process to watch: the locals come in with plastic containers that are filled from a pump. Anyone can buy a plastic container on the spot, which will come with or without a *robinet* (tap), to take it away in. Buying wine *en vrac* (in bulk) in this way is much cheaper but you still have a choice.

Note that if you are going for a large order, you may need to fill in a form and keep a copy with you. This is intended to deter illegal shipping and subsequent bottling for re-sale.

CRU

Somewhat confusingly, this term has two possible meanings when used in connection with wine. *Vin de Cru* is local wine, and the term *Cru* may be used to indicate that the wine comes from a particular area. When used for a Bordeaux wine, however, the term can be taken as a mark of quality. *Cru* is also used as a means of classification, under the usual strict laws imposed in France. This ranges from *Premier Cru* or *Premier Grand Cru*, through *Cru Bourgeois* down to a *Cru Classé*. Any wine that comes within the *Cru* classification will be of good quality, and those that are labelled *Premier Cru* or *Premier Grand Cru* are the finest and therefore the most expensive. Wines marked as *Cru Bourgeois* will also be expensive.

A–Z of French Wine and Drink

A

Abricotine
A liqueur made from brandy and flavoured with apricots.

Absinthe
Another name for wormwood, a bitter herb for flavouring vermouth. Also the name of a liqueur once banned but now back on sale in a less health-hazardous form.

Ambassadeur
Type of *apéritif* made with quinine, gentian, herbs and orange.

Amer Picon
An *apéritif* containing gentian, quinine and orange – the orange is probably to disguise the bitterness of the gentian.

Anisette
A liqueur flavoured with aniseed.

AOC, Appellation d'Origine Contrôlée
A sign that a wine complies with strict government control of the origin and production method (see page 102).

APÉRITIFS

France has an enormous number of apéritifs. Most of them are strongly flavoured with herbs, some of them bitter varieties such as wormwood, and many of them taste like medicines. The best thing to do, if you are curious, is to order one thimbleful in a café and pass it round. One point to remember, however, if you are driving: some of them pack a hefty punch, often containing double the quantity of alcohol in wine, so take a look at the label before ordering another round. The aniseed-based drinks, *pastis* as they are called, such as Pernod and Ricard, turn white and cloudy when water is added to them. Drink them with care, remember their alcohol content is roughly that of whisky, and dilute them well.

Gentian, with a slightly bitter taste, is used to flavour the vivid yellow-coloured Suze; quinine goes into St-Raphael; while Amer Picon contains the lot: gentian, quinine and orange as well. Dubonnet, with its very sweet taste, has gone out of fashion.

Bottles of the local spirit, Calvados, on proud display at this shop in Normandy.

Armagnac

Type of brandy, often of high quality, from the Landes region (see box, page 110).

B

Badoit

One of the best naturally sparkling mineral waters, it is slightly salty and comes from the Loire.

Bénédictine

From Fécamp, Normandy, this was once made there by the monks of that order. It contains not one but several brandies and a mix of herbs.

Bière

Beer. French beer tends to be light-weight, like a lager, unless you are in the Alsace-Lorraine area where the German influence is felt, or near the Belgian border. If you order a beer in a café you will be given the choice of *bouteille* (bottled) or *pression* (from the pump).

Brut

Extra-dry.

Byrrh

A vermouth-like *apéritif*.

C

Café

Coffee (see box, page 109).

Calvados

Type of spirit. Made in Normandy, it has the same status as brandy but is distilled from apples not grapes.

Coffee and a croissant are a traditional start to the day for many French people.

CHOICE OF COFFEE

Select the coffee to suit your taste and you have the basis of the classic continental breakfast or an agreeable after-dinner digestive. Decaffeinated coffee is *décaféiné*, *café crème* is white coffee with milk or cream, as is *café au lait*. *Café nature* and *café noir* are simple plain black coffees, while *café express* is espresso coffee. With a *café filtre*, the coffee is dripped through a filter into a jug or into the cup beneath. *Café gallois* is Irish coffee and *café glacé* is iced coffee. *Café complet* is coffee 'complete' with bread and croissants, a way of ordering breakfast. Usually white coffee is served for breakfast.

There is a tradition in the area to have a *trou Normand*, a tot of Calvados, between courses during a large meal.

Carafe

Decanter, bottle. *Vin en carafe* (decanted wine) is usually an *ordinaire,* and the cheapest on the menu.

Cassis, Crème de

This is an attractive, very sweet liqueur with a deep, mauve-red colour. It is usually served with white wine as a popular *apéritif* known as *vin blanc cassis* or *kir*. *Kir royale* is made with champagne or, occasionally, some other sparkling wine. Cassis is made in the Burgundy region where enormous quantities of blackcurrants are grown. *Sirop de cassis* does not contain alcohol.

Chai

Wine cellar.

Chartreuse

This liqueur is still made by Carthusian monks. It comes in two colours, green and the sweeter yellow type. As well as brandy it is said to contain more than 100 different herbs, and honey too.

Chope

A mug, usually for beer.

Cidre

Cider. It is made mainly in Normandy (though some comes from Brittany) from real old-fashioned cider apples grown around the valley of the Auge. It comes in two versions, still or sparkling (*bouche*). Both have an innocent, light, refreshing taste, but they can take you unawares with their strength. There is also a type of perry made from pears (*poire*).

Citron pressé

Freshly squeezed lemon juice, usually with sugar and water.

COGNAC AND ARMAGNAC

Cognac, the best-known French brandy, distilled from relatively ordinary wine, comes from the area of that name in the Poitou-Charentes. It is sold under famous names such as Martell, Rémy Martin, Courvoisier, Hine and Hennessy.

Armagnac, its less-publicised rival, comes from an area in the Landes, farther south. It is darker in colour and has no brand names that would be immediately recognisable to the average drinker except, perhaps, Janneau. In both cases there are so many varieties that, if you ask simply for a Cognac or Armagnac, you will be presented with a list to choose from. The locals often lace them with fresh grape juice and drink them as an *apéritif*. This drink can be bought bottled as Pineau de Charentes in Cognac and Floc de Gascogne, made in Armagnac.

Cognac

The best-known and arguably the greatest French brandy. It is produced in the *départements* of Charente and Charente-Maritime.

Cointreau

An orange-flavoured liqueur from Angers in the western Loire.

Contrexéville

A still mineral water from the Vosges that has a rather salty flavour.

Curaçao

An orange-flavoured liqueur.

D

Dubonnet

A very sweet, red vermouth-type *apéritif*.

E

Eau de Seltz

Soda water. Sparkling mineral water is usually substituted.

Eau-de-vie

Basically a clear spirit sometimes made with grapes but more often distilled from various fruits. Apples, plums, pears, cherries and more esoteric ingredients, including holly berries and brambles, are all to be found in the form of a fiery spirit. A great many of these drinks are made in mountainous areas such as the Jura and Alsace. Look for a very good one made from pears.

Eau douce

Fresh water.

Eau minérale

Mineral water. There is a large selection of mineral waters in France, and each region tends to be partisan about its own. They can be still (*plate*) or sparkling (*gazeuse*). They range from the very bland, which tastes like fresh spring water, to those with a salty or sharp, almost medicinal, flavour. Everyone makes claims for the efficacy of their waters – Contrexéville, for instance, is supposed to be good for the kidneys – but basically, unless you have a health problem, it simply comes down to personal preference. Perrier, with its distinctive green club-shaped bottle is the best known. However, it is more expensive than many others.

Eau nature

Plain water.

Eau potable

Pure drinking water.

Evian

A still mineral water from the town of that name on Lake Geneva. It has very little taste.

F

Fine

A type of basic, unbranded brandy. It is often drunk *à l'eau* (with

Bottles of Cognac, the most famous of all French brandies.

LIQUEURS

The French have a rather old-fashioned passion for sweet liqueurs and they produce some weird and wonderful concoctions, which look like liquid sweets but can be over 50 per cent proof. The name *crème* is used for sweet liqueurs, for example, *crème de cassis* (blackcurrant), *crème de mûre* (blackberry), or *crème de cacao* (chocolate, made from cocoa beans). Most of these are less exotic and locally made; they do not travel, in that they are probably not on sale out of the area. In general, people either love liqueurs or loathe them. If you like to finish your meal this way, then it is worthwhile experimenting with some new ones. (See under individual entries in this A–Z list.)

water). If you ask for *une fine* in a restaurant, you may well be brought Cognac or Armagnac.

Fraise des bois
An *eau-de-vie* made from wild strawberries.

Framboise
An *eau-de-vie* made from raspberries.

G

Gazeuse
Fizzy water.

Gentiane
A local liqueur from Auvergne, which has a bittersweet taste that not everyone enjoys.

Glaçons
Ice cubes.

Grand Marnier
Orange-flavoured and -coloured liqueur.

Grenadine
Syrup of pomegranate. Used in rum punches and other mixed drinks. Found more in the French Caribbean than in France itself.

Guignolet
Cherry-flavoured spirit from the Loire. It is often thought of as a German or Austrian drink; it is also made in the Haute Saône at Fougerolles, not far from the German border.

K

Kir
Officially, this ubiquitous *apéritif* should be made only with Bourgogne Aligoté white wine and *crème de cassis* liqueur. These days other dry white wines, still or sparkling (*kir royale*), may be used, as may other fruit *crème*

liqueurs such as peach (*pêche*) or blackberry (*mûre*).

Kirsch
Spirit distilled from cherries. It is probably the best-known *eau-de-vie*-type spirit.

M

Marc
Local brandy distilled from grape must. The reputable versions such as *marc de Bourgogne,* made from the last pressings of Burgundy grapes, and *marc de Champagne*, are perfectly safe, but you may be offered, in the spirit of friendship, a glass of 'home brew', distilled from the last of the grape skins and pips; this should be sipped with caution.

Marie Brizard
Originally just an aniseed-based *apéritif* (*pastis*), now a brand name covering a wide range of drinks, such as a lurid-hued violet liqueur.

Myrtilles, crème de
A liqueur flavoured with bilberries.

P

Pernod
Aniseed-based *apéritif* (*pastis*).

Perrier
Mineral water, probably the most famous of them all. It has almost no flavour.

Pichet
A jug or pitcher, usually small in size, of cider or cheap wine, and usually available in *crêperies* or from simple bistros.

Pommeau
A drink from Normandy – Calvados cut with apple juice and served as an *apéritif*. It makes a less alcoholic alternative to pure Calvados.

Pschitt
A brand of lemonade, popular with children.

R

Ricard
Aniseed-based *apéritif* (*pastis*).

S

St-Raphael
Apéritif containing quinine.

Sec
Dry; neat – for example, *whisky sec* is neat whisky.

Supérieur
A term you will find on some Bordeaux bottles – on wines from Graves, for instance. The word does not mean that the wine is superior in quality, but that it contains 1 per cent more alcohol than the official minimum allowed.

Suze
Yellow *apéritif* containing gentian.

T

Tisane

A herbal infusion. The French drink as many, probably even more, *tisanes* than conventional teas, believing that they have a medicinal value. The most popular is probably *tilleul*, lime-flower tea, which is soothing and refreshing. The famous cup of tea with the *madeleine*, which Marcel was drinking at the start of Proust's *À la recherche du temps perdu*, was a *tilleul*.

V

Verveine

Sweet liqueur with bitter undertones, from the Auvergne region.

Vichy

A sparkling water that comes from around the town of that name.

Vin

Wine.

Vin blanc

White wine.

Vin bourru

New wine.

Vin chaud

Mulled wine.

Vin doux

Sweet wine.

Vin du cru or du pays

Local wine, or wine from a particular area.

Vin en carafe

Wine that has been decanted into a container.

Vin en pichet

Wine in a jug – usually a small one.

Vin gris

Pale pink wine – Listel produce a version.

Vin jaune

Yellow wine. From the Jura region. This is a sherry-like dry wine, which is aged in the barrel for at least six years.

Vin mousseux

Sparkling wine, but not made by the *méthode champenoise*.

Vin Muscat

Sweet dessert wine made from Muscat grapes.

Vin ordinaire

Ordinary wine.

Vin rosé

Pink wine.

Vin rouge

Red wine.

Vin sec

Dry wine.

Vittel

A still mineral water from the Nancy area, which has a rather earthy flavour.

Volvic

A well-known still mineral water, which comes from Auvergne and which has no real discernible flavour. It is filtered through volcanic rock.

Eating Out

French dining can be a formal affair, as at this restaurant in Montparnasse, in Paris.

When and Where to Eat

The French have their main meal in the middle of the day, when the shops, factories and schools close, and most people head for home or to the local restaurant to linger over a meal. The vast number and variety of establishments at which you can choose to eat could make the process of selection bewildering, so here's a run-through of what to expect at each.

Hours are more flexible in the larger cities, and there is far more choice of places to eat, whereas in a small town or village it may be difficult to get a snack between meals.

If you are travelling to your destination and staying overnight in a small hotel, your mind may be made up for you, as it may contain the only restaurant in town. Some hotels, on the other hand, do not have a restaurant. In these cases, there will usually be a place to eat nearby. If you are staying in a *chambre d'hôte* (bed and breakfast) you may be able to arrange in advance to have a meal, which often involves dining around a large table with the host family and any other guests.

RESTAURANT

A *restaurant* in France, as in Britain, is the place to go for a full-blown meal. Most display a menu outside including *prix fixe* (set-price) menus at a range of levels, or special *plats du jour* (dishes of the day). Both can be a good, economical choice. Most will also offer a *carte* from which you can select the courses you want, but this is usually a more costly option.

AUBERGE

An *auberge* tends to be a country restaurant, usually combined with a hotel, serving full meals.

HOSTELLERIE

A *hostellerie* is very similar to an *auberge*, and is often housed in an ancient building. However, in large cities, these words can be used to help give a country air to what may be a modern town restaurant.

BISTRO

Going down the social scale, a *bistro* or *bistrot* is a cross between a restaurant and café, the sort of place where you could easily select one course. Service is usually quick and the food cheap but you may be jammed in, for these eateries are usually in premises too small to call themselves restaurants. The table-cloth and napkins may be paper, and you might be expected to keep your cutlery between courses.

BRASSERIE

What began as an alehouse in Alsace is now a term for a bustling, open-all-hours type of place serving traditional food, and good beers as well as wine.

RELAIS ROUTIER

For a good meal at a cheap price but possibly no choice of main dish try a *relais routier*. You might not think of stopping at a pull-up for truckers at home but in France lorry drivers are discerning diners.

CAFÉ

Cafés serve both alcoholic and soft, hot and cold drinks, including delights such as *citron pressé* (fresh lemon juice with water and sugar). You should also be able to get croissants and simple snacks at most of them. It is part of the French way of life to spend anything up to an hour over one drink in a café, so the waiter will not hassle you. Equally, if you want to get away quickly, pay for your drink when he brings it to you, or you may have difficulty in catching his eye for the bill. In villages, the café often doubles as the *tabac* (tobac-conist), but even these are now non-smoking – unless, perhaps, you are in a truly off-the-beaten-track place.

When the weather is good, what could be better than outdoor dining in Paris?

Savoury or sweet, crêpes make a quick and filling meal.

SALON DE THÉ

A *salon de thé* is usually quite an elegant place in a shopping area, sometimes attached to a *pâtisserie*, where you can order rather weak tea and try some delicious cakes. The tea will be served with lemon, incidentally, unless you specifically ask for milk. The word for tea is '*thé*', while *thé au citron* is lemon tea, and *thé à la menthe* – if you want to try it – is peppermint tea, which is reckoned to be good for the digestion. A wide range of other flavoured teas (*tisanes*) have also become fashionable.

BUFFET

If you are taking a meal out of normal eating hours, while travelling, for instance, you can always get a meal in a *buffet* at a train station. It might be the last thing you would think of doing at home, but in France some first-class meals can be had at a station *buffet*, and many are even Michelin-rated.

BAR OR BISTRO À VINS

In Paris and the main wine regions, these places will offer good wine by the glass or bottle, and food such as platters of local cheese or *charcuterie*.

DRUG STORES

In the larger towns, drug stores serve meals at all times. The words *casse-croûte* mean snack and if the words *à toutes heures* are alongside them, you know you are in luck, because food is served at all hours.

QUICK AND CHEAP

If you are in a hurry, merely using food as fuel, or having to count the euros carefully, then head for the *libre-service* (self-service) cafeterias located in the supermarkets, or on the autoroutes.

Pizza places can be found all over France, and *crêperies* are a good choice for a quick cheap meal. Fast food chains have opened up all over the country too.

If you just want a drink and a sandwich, then look for a *buvette*, where you will probably stand up to eat or take your purchase away with you. Never insult the proprietor of a full-blown restaurant by saying you are in a hurry – he or she simply would not understand your attitude.

If you are on the move, and do not want to stop for long, then it is best to take a picnic lunch with you rather than queue up at a crowded *libre-service* or have a long wait in a restaurant.

Though the motorway cafés do not go in for great cuisine, the food is perfectly adequate, inexpensive and the service is quick – usually you will find both a restaurant and a snack bar.

FOR BREAKFAST

You may be served with the traditional French breakfast at your hotel as part of the price of your room for the night. *Café complet*, as it is called, varies according to the standard of the hotel and the price of the room, from fresh orange juice, a basket of croissants and *brioches* plus a choice of *confiture*, to reheated *café* with milk and toasted pieces of yesterday's bread with no choice of jam.

If you haven't paid for breakfast in advance, and it looks disappointing, then simply take yourselves off to the nearest café and have your breakfast there. The croissants are sure to be fresh and still warm, and the coffee better.

OPENING TIMES

An excellent tip for discovering what the restaurant opening hours are is to keep an eye on the local shops; as they close for lunch the restaurants will open. In general, a good restaurant fills up fast and early for lunch. It's not excessive to turn up at noon at a particularly popular place if you want to be sure of a table.

In the south, meals tend to be served a little later in the evening than elsewhere in France. This means that if you have a small child with you, you may find it difficult to get anything to eat in the evening before 7pm.

At the Restaurant

One of the great pleasures of holidaying in France is to linger over a meal in a restaurant after a busy day. Some of your most memorable meals are likely to be taken in a quiet country backwater, rather than in a busy city where parking may be difficult and prices high.

BOOKING A TABLE

There is nothing more disappointing than to arrive at the restaurant of your choice only to find it is *complet* (full). So if you are planning a special meal out, it is as well to phone and book in advance (your hotel will do it if necessary). Sunday lunchtime is a favourite with French families for taking a meal out, especially in the country, so it is important to book then; also book on public holidays and other days that may catch you unawares, such as Bastille Day (14 July), for instance, when the whole town will go out *en fête* with brass bands, fireworks, the lot, and everyone eats out *en famille*.

Remember to be prompt if you reserve a table; if you are more than, say, 10 minutes late, your table is likely to have been given to someone else. Apart from in the most formal restaurants, the dress code is relaxed. Smoking is banned in all indoor public areas. Disabled access may be limited and it is worthwhile mentioning any special needs when you book.

Lunch is the main meal of the day for most French people.

THE MENU

Having chosen your restaurant, you will need to make your choice of food, either choosing the most expensive way, from *à la carte* dishes shown on the *carte* (menu), or from the *table d'hôte* (literally, the table of the host), a menu with a smaller choice. There may be a range of *prix fixe* menus too, which offer a choice of courses. Go for the *plat du jour* or the *spécialité de la maison* if you want to try something local.

Many restaurants will also have a *menu touristique,* 'safe' food at a reasonable price – probably pork chop or steak and *frites* (chips). For those who want a real blow-out, however, try the *menu gastronomique,* the most expensive one on the *carte*, with extra courses and more flamboyant food.

If you see no price but the letters *SG* (*selon grosseur*) against a dish – often something such as lobster – then it is sold by size or weight, and it is as well to ask the price in advance.

Lunch menus can be very good value, giving you the chance to dine at a top-flight restaurant where dinner would be astronomical. Vegetarian dishes remain a rarity except in university towns. Cheese is served as a separate course before, or instead of, dessert.

By law, all menus should show prices that include taxes and service, but it is still the norm to leave a tip of up to 10 per cent for good service, good food and a welcoming atmosphere.

On the drinks front, unless you want something special, the *vin de pays* or *vin de table* is usually a perfectly adequate, inexpensive choice of wine. If you order *eau minérale* they will want to know if you want it *gazeuse* (sparkling) or *non-gazeuse*. But don't feel ashamed to ask for a simple *carafe d'eau*, which will be a jug of tap water.

Children

It seems a shame to take children abroad without giving them a chance to enjoy local regional food. Children can have amazingly sophisticated tastes – I have known toddlers who loved *moules marinière* and *escargots* (snails), for instance. It is often the older child who is more finicky. So it is a good idea to prepare the children in advance by adding one or two French dishes to their ordinary menu at home, to acclimatise them. It is a good idea, too, to take them out for a meal or two back home, if they are not used to eating in restaurants.

Children are generally accepted anywhere in France, though if you are going to a really high-class restaurant it is as well to check first that a child will be welcome. It probably will be fine, though a certain standard of behaviour will be expected – playing hide and seek among the tables, for instance, would definitely not be appreciated.

If you are travelling with a small, very active child, you probably will not want to eat in the hushed silence of a grand restaurant anyway – even though the proprietor will probably come rushing up with a number of *coussins* (cushions) or a high-chair.

French children seem to have an inbuilt attitude towards meals that makes them able to sit gravely through a four-course dinner with *grandpère* and *grandmère*, while ours would grizzle, whine and want to get down. So if you are dealing with a fractious, travel-tired toddler and are worried about behaviour problems, make it easy for everyone and either choose a self-service or fast-food place or, better still, a restaurant with tables in the garden, where they can run round as much as they like, while you enjoy a meal. Certainly a place that has paper tablecloths rather than the damask variety is less nerve-racking.

If necessary, order a plate of chips (*frites*) immediately, or a strategic ice-cream (*glace*) for the child while you are still on your main course. The French will quite understand.

Despite the fact that French water is perfectly drinkable, a possible tummy upset for a toddler is not worth the risk, so it may be safer to stick with a brand of still mineral water.

Eating In

Shopping for food, such as delicious French bread, is part of the fun of a French holiday.

Shopping

There is a huge diversity of shopping in France. On the one hand there are some of the largest supermarkets outside of the US and, at the other end of the scale, tiny delightful *marchés* (markets), with a stall or two set up under some trees to sell local produce.

It would be a shame to go on holiday and take refuge in supermarkets and markets alone when France has so many superb specialist shops. The sensible way to shop is to buy functional items such as washing powder at the supermarket, then use the specialist shops for food.

ALIMENTATION GÉNÉRALE

Alimentation Générale is the sign that you will see over a shop that sells dairy goods, groceries and a basic range of household products.

BOUCHERIE

The *boucherie* is the butcher's shop and sells all kinds of meat, although pork is not sold in *boucheries* in the south. Cuts of meat in France are different from those in butcher's shops elsewhere, and the meat is usually cut specially for each customer. You will never see mince, for instance, out on display; instead, a choice piece of beef will be specially put through the mincer for you. Meat, particularly lamb, is expensive, but of a high quality with no wastage, so you need not buy too much. Some butchers sell cooked food, including ready-roasted chickens and items of *charcuterie* – the smaller the town or village, the wider the range.

A *boucherie chevaline* sells horse meat – you will usually find a horse's head sign above the door.

BOULANGERIE

The *boulangerie*, the bakery, is the most important shop in any village. There is one open every day of the week because, by French law, every village over a certain size must have a baker or a supplier of bread. And the bread (see box, opposite) is baked at least twice a day to ensure that it is absolutely fresh. A *dépôt de pain* sells bread not baked on the premises. A village too tiny to have its own shop will be visited by a bread van at least once a day.

The *boulangerie* also sells the staple items of the French breakfast: the classic crescent-shaped *croissants* and the delicious *pains au chocolat*, *brioches* and many other kinds of buns. The *boulangerie* in a small village will also sell gâteaux, fruit tarts and, often, quiches and pizzas.

CHARCUTERIE

The *charcuterie*, once simply a pork butcher, now tends to sell all sorts of delicatessen items, and this is the place to plunder for a picnic. Essentially, it is a cooked meat shop, although it sells pork ready for cooking as well. Here you will find pâtés, terrines and *saucisses*,

DAILY BREAD

The familiar French loaf is bought fresh every day quite simply because it becomes stale very quickly. The light texture of the bread, made from a soft flour, and its long, thin shape contribute to this. In French households, bread left over at the end of the day is likely to be placed in the bottom of the soup tureen or dunked in coffee the next day.

The thinnest loaf, known as a *ficelle*, is also shorter than the long, comparatively plump *baguette*. *Un baton*, *un pain* or *une gresson* are also names you are likely to encounter for similar, long loaves, and the thickest are called *Parisien* or *gros pain*. *Petit pain* is the short version (a large roll) and *pain épi* is a useful loaf for picnics, as it is a long stick made corn-ear style. The crunchy points of dough on *pain épi* may be broken away easily, like a series of linked bread rolls. Wholemeal and brown bread is known variously as *pain de son*, *pain de siègle*, *pain bis*, *pain complet* or *pain entier*. *Pain noir* is also a term for wholemeal bread. Soft-crusted bread, of the type often sliced for sandwiches, is known as *pain de mie*. Oval, soft-crumbled crusty loaves are *Viennois*, and rings of bread (of the same type as *baguettes*) are *couronnes*. A round, slightly flattened loaf, the *pain campagne*, is not as light as a stick and stays fresh for longer. You will also find delicious breads with nuts or olives in them, or with cheese on top. Then there are the familiar rich breads – the *croissant*, *brioche* and *pain au chocolat* (*croissant*-like dough made into buns with chocolate in the middle).

Chocolate shops are of the highest quality.

from the air-dried variety to those that need cooking. Look out for items such as *rillons*, *rillettes* and pigs' ears in jelly. There will be black and white puddings (*boudin blanc* and *noir*), *andouillettes* and the spicy hot *merguez* sausages as well as frankfurters, also hams and galantines. There will be salad items including *céleri remoulade* and *champignons à la grecque*, and probably small quiches and pizzas.

The *charcuterie* will often sell made-up dishes too, or ready-cooked meals to take away – or look for these in the *traiteur* (take-away food shop). These foods usually include dishes such as couscous, *choucroute*, ready-roasted chickens and at least one *plat du jour* – a *daube*, for instance.

If you are buying ham, avoid *jambon de Paris* or *jambon de York*, both of which tend to be tasteless; look for local hams instead. You may even find *jambon de marcassin*, which is an elegant ham made from smoked wild boar.

CONFISERIE

The *confiserie* is the sweet shop, selling quality hand-made chocolates and bon-bons, nougat and crystallised fruit. Sometimes the *confiserie* forms part of a tea-room or a *pâtisserie*. The best buy from here is undoubtedly chocolate – at a price, though, with truffles topping the bill. At Easter time the *confiserie* shops are full of chocolate rabbits, chickens and nests of eggs. If you buy one of these it will be elaborately gift-wrapped for you.

ÉPICERIE

The *épicerie* is the grocery, often also called the *Alimentation Générale*. Except in very small villages, it is run along the lines of a supermarket, but with a counter for items such as cheese and unpackaged meats.

FROMAGERIE

The *fromagerie* is a specialist cheese shop, usually found only in larger towns. There are hundreds of French cheeses to choose from, some of which are listed in the A–Z of French Food.

You are never expected to buy your cheese in a *fromagerie* without tasting it first – that would be unheard of. Two types of cheese you might like to try are *fromage fort*, a fermented cheese usually flavoured with herbs, and *fromage frais*, which you will find in all shops and supermarkets. The latter is a yoghurt-like fresh 'cheese' with a bland taste. It is soft and used instead of cream with fruit.

MARCHÉ

Street markets are part of the French way of life, and in every self-respecting town, one day of the week is market day – frequently Saturday. Enquire at the local *Syndicat d'Initiative* (tourist office). Apart from that, even the smallest village will have a few stalls set out, including, perhaps, a visit from the *charcuterie* or *poissonnerie* van and a cheese vendor on one special day a week.

Stalls selling olives are fascinating, too, with more than a dozen different types on offer – including delicious tiny varieties. Local housewives also set up pavement stalls to sell their own produce, usually honey or jam – expensive but excellent. Look out for unusual conserves such as lemon and ginger. Travelling organic vegetable vans that tour the villages are now also becoming part of the scene.

Markets are the best places to buy fresh flowers, fruit and vegetables in season. There will almost certainly also be kitchen utensils and gadgets, crockery and cutlery. So this is the place to buy the corkscrew, the knife and any picnicking item that you forgot to pack. Markets are a good place for children, too, as there is plenty to do and see – often a hurdy-gurdy man or a puppeteer to entertain them, or even a roundabout. Depending on their age, children may either be delighted or appalled by stalls selling live rabbits and hens, but they are being sold for breeding rather than for the pot.

Even if your French is not all that it should be, you can get by at the market by mime – pointing, prodding and smiling. It is quite in order to ask to taste (*goûter*) a sliver of cheese, pâté or sausage, just as it is to pick out the particular fruit or vegetables that you want from a market stall. When buying foods such as pâté, it is better to ask for *une tranche* (a slice) rather than so many grams, or say you are buying for 'x' number of *personnes* and leave it to the good sense of the stall holder. When it comes to fruit and vegetables, more and more market stalls and shops now provide plastic baskets or bags on display at the front. You simply help yourself, the assistant weighs it up and tells you how much it costs. When buying produce that ripens, from cheese to fruit, you may well be asked when you plan to eat it so that you can be sold an item at just the right stage for your needs.

MINI-SUPERMARKET

In small towns or larger villages you should find a grocery shop, usually franchised from chains such as Casino, Shopi and Super U. They are almost always set out on supermarket lines and are a practical place to shop for anyone whose French is non-existent or rather rusty. It is so much easier to help yourself to things rather than look up the words for items. You will find that the proprietor will be chatty and friendly, especially when he or she gets to know you. Many have fruit and vegetables as well as grocery items and drinks.

PÂTISSERIE

The *pâtisserie* sells cakes both large and small and, above all, impressive-looking tarts and flans that are bought for dessert in a French home as a matter of course. There will be delicious biscuits, too. Look out for *babas* (*baba au rhum*)

and *savarins* drowned in liqueurs, as well as *madeleines*, meringues and gâteaux such as *St-Honoré* and *pithiviers*. The *pâtisserie* is also very often an ice-cream maker, and you may be able to buy some splendid sorbets, particularly fruit-flavoured versions.

POISSONNERIE

The *poissonnier,* the fishmonger, very often operates from a stall or van, rather than from a shop. There is, as you would expect, an enormous range of fish to be had in France, even far inland. It is here that you will find a tray heaped with all kinds of tiny fish labelled *soupe de poisson.* A kilo of these will make mouthwatering soup in no time at all (see recipe, pages 133–4). Look out for plump fresh sardines to grill out of doors and steaks of fresh tuna (*thon*), which are filling enough to take the place of a hearty meat meal. Try your hand with swordfish (*espadon*), octopus (*poulpe*) or mussels (*moules*).

You will also find salted cod (*morue*) on sale, which needs soaking for 24 hours in many changes of water before use. It is used in a classic Provençal dish *aïoli garni,* something of an acquired taste, which combines salted cod, vegetables and a garnish of snails.

It used to be eaten on Fridays only but is now on the menu all through the week.

SUPERMARKETS AND HYPERMARKETS

The supermarkets and hyper-markets are mainly out of town, the latter being vast drive-in complexes where you can eat, park the children in a crèche, have your hair done, buy furniture, sports gear and, of course, food. It is certainly the cheapest place to stock up with basic goods if you are catering for yourself. Names to look out for (they usually advertise themselves with huge hoardings on the highways) are Auchan, Intermarché, Carrefour (one of the largest and most widespread) and Leclerc, which is often cheaper than the others. They usually stay open late in the evening, up to 9 or 10pm. In the holiday areas, their opening hours tend to change with the seasons, shutting for a siesta at midday in summer. Traditionally closed on Sundays, it is increasingly easy to find a *supermarché* (often Intermarché) open on a Sunday morning.

Supermarkets are useful if it is raining, when the idea of wandering round the *marché* does not appeal. You also have time to price items at your leisure and to read the labels on the products. When you get to the check-out, the cashier will tell you the total – difficult to hear and understand quickly. So keep an eye on the till where the figures will be displayed. Every supermarket now accepts chip-and-pin cards, which makes the business of paying much easier. For small amounts, do not be afraid to spread out the change in your hand and let the cashier help him or herself to the bits and pieces.

TRAITEUR

The *traiteur* is the busy person's friend, the take-away food shop, where you can buy ready-prepared, often ready-cooked foods, including quite elaborate dishes. This is a good way to try the local speci-alities of the region if you are in self-catering accommodation. Then, if you like what you taste, you can look up the recipe, and try it at home.

OTHER FOOD SHOPS

There are a few other shops you may encounter, such as a *volailler*, the poulterer; *crémerie*, selling dairy products and – though less and less as time goes by – a *triperie*, selling tripe with a range of sauces. Health food shops are now widespread in France (see Special Diets, pages 130–31).

NON-FOOD SHOPS

Other, non-food, shops you may need are the *pharmacie*, the chemist, which does not always sell cosmetic items or soaps. Toiletry items are more likely to be found at the *droguerie*, a type of hardware store.

If you are in need of a dry-cleaning service, look out for the sign *nettoyage à sec. Une blanchisserie* is a laundry. *Un tabac*, the tobacconist, with its distinctive red cigar-shaped sign over the door, sells stamps and possibly postcards as well as cigarettes and cigars. A *maison de la presse* sells newspapers and magazines, while a *librairie* is a bookshop, not a library – that is, a *bibliothèque*. The weird-looking word *quincaillerie*, by the way, denotes a hardware shop.

WHEN TO SHOP

Shopping hours vary according to what part of France you are in. In general, most shops open around 8.30am, then close at noon until about 2.30 or as late as 3.30–4pm during the summer in the tourist areas, when they will stay open until 6.30–7pm. Some hyper-markets stay open at lunchtime – a good time to shop, because the French take their main meal of the day at lunchtime, they are almost always half-empty. Most shops, and

all banks, are closed on Monday. Banks also have different opening times on a Saturday and are closed on national holidays.

CHILDREN

Travelling with a child in France is no more difficult than anywhere else. Most of the popular brands of food can be found in the supermarkets. And for older children, foodstuffs such as cornflakes and ketchup are also becoming available.

If you are self-catering, once installed in your villa or *gîte*, let the older children do some simple shopping, for example, going to the *boulangerie* to get the breakfast bread. Encourage them to learn a few words of French, even if it is only *bonjour* and *au revoir*. They will also enjoy visits to the market, and comparing French names of familiar items in supermarkets. Very small children overcome the language barrier of their own accord and love to play with French children of their own age. Above all, remember that the French love children, so relax!

SPECIAL DIETS

If you are on a special diet of any kind, gluten-free, for instance, then you ought to try to pack basic food to take with you to France. However, many hypermarkets now have a dazzling range of products for special diets. If you are worried about cholesterol counts or simply trying to lose weight, low-fat products are now widely available in supermarkets. Even the famous crème fraîche can be bought in a low-fat version that tastes just the same as the ordinary kind, and there are low-fat yoghurts around too. You can also buy frozen ready-to-heat diet meals in the shops.

Anyone who enjoys herbal tea will find that France has almost as varied a selection of tisanes, as they are called, as of wine. You find them in pharmacies, in health food shops or increasingly in specialist tea vendors. Also look out for them at the local market, the traditional place for selling the ingredients for drinks of this kind. On a stall there will be little sacks of lime flowers (tillleul), of lemon verbena

(verveine), and dried fruits too, such as blackcurrants (cassis), and camomile, of course. Cherry stalks (queues de cerises) are a useful natural diuretic, while mint (menthe) is good for the digestion.

Vegans, vegetarians or anyone with special dietary wishes should be able to buy most items they require from health food shops called centres diététiques or aliments naturels.

A point to watch out for if you are on a low-salt diet – some of the classic French mineral waters have a high salt content. The amount can easily be discovered by reading the bottle labels carefully. The popular Evian and the lesser-known Charrier, if you can find it, are both sodium-free. Evian has a slight diuretic effect; so does Contrexéville.

A trip to a bustling French market is a must.

Recipes

PETIT CHÈVRE CHAUD
GOATS' MILK CHEESE STARTER

SERVES FOUR

This fashionable starter is made with goats' milk cheese but you could substitute another soft cheese such as Camembert. Two portions per person make a good lunch.

1 cylindrical goats' milk cheese, such as Ste-Maure
2 tablespoons chopped fresh herbs, such as thyme, marjoram or chives
250ml/8fl oz *sauce vinaigrette*
2 tablespoons chopped walnuts (optional)
mixed green salad

Slice the cheese into four thick rounds, place on a baking tray and sprinkle with herbs. Put the cheese under a hot grill (or in a hot oven if you are without a grill). Set to one side to keep warm while you heat the *vinaigrette* just to blood temperature. Sprinkle the walnuts over the salad and serve it on four plates. Spoon a little warm *vinaigrette* over, then top with the cheese.

Goats' milk cheese with dressed salad.

SOUPE AU PISTOU
HEARTY VEGETABLE SOUP
WITH BASIL PASTE

SERVES FOUR

A famous vegetable soup from Nice, pistou is a corruption of the Italian word pesto, a paste made with basil, which gives the soup its special flavour. Traditionally you should include pine nuts (pignons), Italian-style, in the basil paste. The haricots must be fresh, not dried. If fresh haricots are unavailable, substitute canned.

2 tablespoons oil
1 onion, skinned and sliced
2 tomatoes, skinned and chopped
salt and freshly ground black pepper
250g/9oz fresh haricot beans
250g/9oz green beans
1 courgette, chopped
2 large sticks of celery, chopped
2 potatoes, peeled and chopped
50g/2oz *vermicelli*
For the pistou
8 sprigs of fresh basil
2 cloves garlic, skinned
½ tablespoon pine nuts
2 tablespoons olive oil
1 tablespoon grated Parmesan cheese

Heat the oil in a large pan, add the onion and cook gently until golden in colour – about 20 minutes or more. Stir in the chopped tomatoes, season, then add about 750ml/1¼ pints water and bring to the boil. Add the haricot beans and simmer for 10 minutes, then put in the green beans, courgette, celery and potatoes. Leave to simmer for 30 minutes.

Meanwhile make the *pistou*: pound the basil leaves together with garlic and pine nuts in a pestle and mortar or blender. Add the oil, drop by drop, then mix in the grated Parmesan. When the soup is ready, add the vermicelli and bring it back to the boil. Take a cupful of soup mixture, stir in the *pistou* sauce, then return it to the pan. Simmer for 5 minutes and serve.

SOUPE DE POISSON
FISH SOUP

SERVES 6

The saffron gives this soup its traditional yellow-red colour. The fish mix, simply known as soupe de poisson, *must include the* rascasse, *a small ugly red fish. To prepare this soup properly, you need a Mouli sieve to filter out the bones. This soup is served with* aïoli *or* rouille, *toasted French bread and cheese.*

1kg/2lb mixed small fish
3–4 tablespoons olive oil
2 cloves garlic, skinned and crushed
2 onions, skinned and sliced
2 Marmande-type or beef tomatoes, roughly chopped, plus 2 large tomatoes, chopped
a large piece of fennel, sliced
sprig of parsley
¼ teaspoon saffron strands
1 bay leaf
300ml/½ pint dry white wine
125g/4½oz *vermicelli*, broken into short lengths
salt and freshly ground black pepper
slices of toasted French bread
75g/3oz grated Gruyère cheese
For the rouille
2 slices French bread
2 cloves garlic
¼ teaspoon salt
2 canned red peppers or 2 red chillies, seeded and chopped
olive oil

Wash and pick over the fish. Scale the larger pieces and gut them if necessary but leave heads and tails on the small fish. Heat the oil in a large pan and fry the garlic and onion for a few moments. Stir in the tomatoes, fennel, parsley, then the fish, together with a few strands of saffron and the bay leaf. Meanwhile pound the remaining saffron to a powder. Stir the fish mixture well and cook over a medium heat for five minutes, gently crushing the saffron strands as the mixture cooks. Add 2 litres/3½ pints water, the wine and powdered saffron. Bring to the boil and simmer, uncovered, for 20 minutes, skimming off any froth. Take out the bay leaf, then pass the mixture through a Mouli sieve (you can use a blender and a sieve if you do not have a Mouli, but the effect is not quite the same). Bring the soup back to the boil, add the *vermicelli*, adjust the seasoning, and cook for a further 15 minutes.

To make the *rouille*, soak the bread in a little water for five minutes. Then squeeze it dry until it is like a wrung-out flannel. Crush the garlic with the salt, peppers or chillies and bread in a pestle and mortar. Add oil gradually until you have a thick paste. Serve the soup piping hot with bowls of grated Gruyère and *rouille*. Traditionally you then spread toasted slices of French bread with the *rouille*, then float them on the top, either sprinkling cheese over the soup itself or over the toast.

SALADE NIÇOISE
VEGETABLE SALAD WITH OLIVES AND ANCHOVIES

SERVES FOUR

Everyone has a favourite version of salade niçoise. Depending on what you put in it, this salad can serve as a filling lunch dish or just as an attractive starter. But common to every version are two things – olives and anchovies. This version below would make a fairly filling lunch. If you want it to be even more substantial, add some cooked young artichoke hearts and chunks of canned tuna. Though not a traditional ingredient, lettuce – preferably the crisp type – can also be added.

Salade niçoise *is a perennial and very adaptable favourite.*

1 clove garlic, skinned and cut in half

2 eggs

½ cucumber

500g/1lb tomatoes, skinned and quartered

1 red or green pepper, seeded and sliced

handful of cooked French beans, cut into short lengths

1 medium onion, skinned and sliced

salt and freshly ground black pepper

1 (50g/2oz) can anchovies

12 black olives, stoned

4 tablespoons *sauce vinaigrette*, preferably made with tarragon vinegar

1 tablespoon chopped fresh parsley

Rub the inside of a wooden salad bowl with the cut clove of garlic. Hard-boil the eggs. Then plunge them into cold water to stop the yolks from blackening, before shelling them and setting them aside to cool. Next, skin the cucumber using a potato peeler or sharp knife, then chop it by slicing it down the length into four 'planks' and cutting across. Put the other prepared vegetables in the salad bowl, season well with salt and pepper.

Drain the anchovies and cut the fillets in half lengthways and add both to the salad with the olives. Spoon over the *vinaigrette* and toss the salad. Quarter the eggs and arrange them on top. Sprinkle with parsley and serve with French bread.

GRATIN DAUPHINOIS
GRATIN OF POTATOES BAKED IN MILK

SERVES FOUR

This can be used as either a main or a side dish. French potatoes tend to be waxy, which is why they are so difficult to purée. This delicious potato dish makes the most of their ability to maintain their shape. Part-cooking the potatoes in a saucepan speeds up the cooking time of this dish, which can otherwise take as long as 2 hours. You can, if you prefer, simply arrange the potato pieces in an earthenware dish, dot them with butter, pour in the milk and mix, then cook the gratin for 1¾ to 2 hours in a warm oven. Gruyère is often sold ready-grated in packets in French supermarkets. To make a main course for lunch, add more than the suggested 50g/2oz of cheese.

500g/1lb potatoes, peeled

250ml/8fl oz milk

50g/2oz unsalted butter

250ml/8fl oz cream or *crème fraîche*

salt and freshly ground black pepper

grated nutmeg

1 clove garlic

25g/1oz butter, to grease

50g/2oz Gruyère cheese, grated

Slice the potatoes thinly into rounds, using the slicing attachment of a food processor or a *mandoline*, if you have one. Rinse them well to get rid of excess starch as this will make them stick together. Bring the milk to the boil in a large pan. Stir in the unsalted butter, potatoes and cream, then season with salt, pepper and grated nutmeg to taste. Stir carefully with a wooden spoon, separating the potato slices as you go. Bring slowly to the boil and cook over a low heat for 30 minutes.

Set the oven at 160°C, 325°F, gas 3. Meanwhile, rub the interior of an earthenware dish with the garlic, then butter the sides of the dish. Pour in the potato mix and sprinkle the top with the grated Gruyère. Cook in the oven for about 45 minutes. If you like, put the dish under the grill for a minute or two to brown the top to a deep golden colour.

PIPÉRADE
SCRAMBLED EGGS WITH PEPPERS

SERVES FOUR

This quick, easy and cheap lunch dish from the Basque country is a scrambled version of a Spanish omelette. You can add other ingredients – chopped ham, for instance, or pieces of bacon, or chopped cooked potato – to make the dish even more filling. Incorporate these extra ingredients at the same time as the onion and, if necessary, add a little more oil. If you prefer, substitute a green pepper in place of one of the red ones.

2 red peppers, seeded
8 eggs
salt and freshly ground black pepper
2 tablespoons olive oil
1 large onion, skinned and chopped
2 cloves garlic, skinned and crushed
500g/1lb tomatoes, skinned and chopped

Slice the peppers into strips, then chop them into shorter lengths. Beat the eggs together in a bowl with a little salt and pepper.

Heat the oil in a large, heavy pan and cook the onion over a low heat until it is golden brown. Stir in the garlic, then push the mixture to one side. Tilt the pan so that the oil runs down, then add the peppers and cook them for a minute or two. Add the tomatoes and stir the vegetables together. Cook over a low heat for about 8 minutes or until they have all softened, some of the moisture has evaporated and the mixture has firmed up a little.

Pour in the eggs, and stir them in. Continue to cook the mixture, stirring gently (do not overdo it or it will go an unpleasant grey-brown colour). The moment the underneath is set and the top is thick and creamy, take the pan off the heat and allow the *pipérade* to finish cooking by its own heat. Serve with crusty French bread.

The ingredients for a memorable ratatouille *should be easy to find.*

RATATOUILLE
PROVENÇAL VEGETABLE RAGOÛT

SERVES SIX

A great Provençal dish that is, basically, a mix of vegetables stewed in olive oil. It can be eaten hot or cold, as a side dish or a main course – with fried eggs on top, for instance, for lunch. Ratatouille even improves after a night spent in the refrigerator. The essential ingredients are tomatoes, aubergines (eggplants), onions, peppers, courgettes, garlic and olive oil. But you can vary the recipe by adding mushrooms or even olives.

2 aubergines (eggplants)
2 courgettes
3 large tomatoes
6 tablespoons olive oil
3 large onions, skinned and chopped
2 large peppers, seeded and sliced
2 cloves garlic, skinned and crushed

Prepare the aubergines ahead of time. First, cut them into thick half-moons. Sprinkle with salt, then put them in a colander with a weighted plate on top. Leave to drain over a bowl or in the sink. Next, cut the courgettes into rounds. Skin the tomatoes by nicking their skins, then plunging them into boiling water and leaving them there for a moment. Remove the skins, then chop the tomatoes.

Heat the oil in a large heavy pan with a lid and fry the aubergine until it has coloured. Add the peppers, onion and garlic, and allow them to soften. Then add the courgettes. Finally, add the chopped tomatoes. When the mixture is bubbling, put the lid back on the pan, turn down the heat and simmer until soft – about 45 minutes.

Serve hot one day with crusty bread, cold the next.

Seafood dishes can be very simple if the ingredients are good.

COQUILLES ST-JACQUES AU GRATIN

SCALLOP GRATIN

SERVES FOUR

Coquilles St-Jacques (scallops) can be cooked very simply in their shells just by dotting them with butter and bread-crumbs and cooking them in the oven for about 20 minutes. This recipe is a little more elaborate and makes a more filling dish. If you are making it at home, from frozen scallops, you can serve the scallops in large ramekins if you do not have any shells.

8 scallops in their shells
450ml/15fl oz milk
25g/1oz butter
4 tablespoons plain flour
75g/3oz hard cheese, finely grated
salt and freshly ground black pepper
2 tablespoons double cream or *crème fraîche* (optional)
For the topping
50g/2oz breadcrumbs
25g/1oz hard cheese, grated

Prise open the scallops and remove the black *sac*. Scrub and dry four deep shells. Trim the white part of the scallops then rinse and drain it along with the red coral. Cut into small pieces and season. Place in a saucepan with the milk and simmer for two minutes or until just firm. Drain, reserving the milk, and keep warm.

Melt the butter in another pan, add the flour, and cook for 2 minutes, stirring carefully to avoid browning. Lower the heat and gradually stir in the reserved milk. Bring to the boil and cook until the sauce thickens, stirring all the time. Stir in the 75g/3oz cheese, then check the seasoning. If the sauce becomes lumpy blend it or beat with a wire whisk.

Next, pile the scallops back into the four cleaned shells. Stir the cream or *crème fraîche* into the sauce and gener-ously coat the scallops with it. Sprinkle with a mix of the breadcrumbs and cheese for the topping. Then brown under a hot grill.

CASSOULET

HARICOT BEAN CASSEROLE
WITH PORK AND LAMB

SERVES SIX

The name comes from cassol, *the
southwestern French dialect word for
the clay cooking pot traditionally used.
Eat* cassoulet, *and you realise why the
French make lunch the main meal of
the day, for it is far too heavy to digest
in the evening. This dish improves on
reheating. It is vital to use real white
haricot beans to obtain the right flavour.
Preserved goose (*confit d'oie*) is widely
sold in food shops throughout France.*

500g/1lb white haricot beans
175g/6oz salt pork or a chunk of
    unsmoked bacon, such as knuckle
500g/1lb belly pork or pork spare rib, in
    large pieces
2 cloves garlic, skinned and crushed
bouquet garni
1 carrot, peeled
1 whole onion, skinned and stuck with
    6 cloves
salt and freshly ground black pepper
50g/2oz goose fat or lard
350g/12oz preserved goose (*confit
    d'oie*)
1 onion, skinned and chopped
350g/12oz boned shoulder of lamb, cut
    into large chunks
250g/9oz garlic sausage or other similar
    sausage, cut into chunks
75g/3oz white breadcrumbs

Soak the haricot beans for an hour to
soften them. Cut off any rind from the
salt pork or bacon and belly or spare rib
pork. Chop the rind into squares and set
it aside for the time being.

Put the beans and salt pork or bacon
in a large saucepan together with the
garlic, *bouquet garni*, carrot and the
onion stuck with cloves. Season,
cover with water and simmer for
1½ hours.

Meanwhile, heat the goose fat in a
frying pan and brown the preserved
goose and chopped onion. Remove
from the pan, then brown the belly pork
and lamb pieces, adding a little extra fat
if necessary. Reserve any remaining fat
at the end of cooking.

Set the oven at 160°C, 325°F, gas
3. Remove the clove-studded onion

*French cooking is synonymous with the
use of garlic.*

A delicious meal of couscous is not complete without spicy harissa.

from the saucepan and, using a slotted spoon, put the reserved bacon or pork rind in the base of a large earthenware pot with a close-fitting lid. Cover with a layer of beans, meats, then more beans, then meat, topping the dish with chunks of garlic sausage. Moisten the contents with some of the cooking broth. Cover and cook in the oven for 1½ hours, adding more broth occasionally if necessary to keep the mixture moist.

Finally, take the lid off the pot and sprinkle the top with the white bread-crumbs. Pour a little reserved goose fat from the frying pan over the top. Put the pot back in the oven uncovered for another 20 minutes, or until the top has formed a golden crust. Serve on its own.

COUSCOUS

SERVES FOUR TO SIX

The sign 'Couscous aujourd'hui' is found hanging in the windows of cafés and brasseries all over France. It signifies that the North African dish is being served, usually for lunch. The reason for its popularity is France's colonial history, linked as it is to Algeria and Morocco. Couscous is extremely filling and very tasty. If you want a lighter dish, or want to save cash, remove the chicken and lamb from the recipe, add green peppers and aubergines (eggplants) and you have couscous aux sept légumes instead. The couscous itself, which is actually rolled semolina, can be found in shops in an easy cook (toute prête) version all over France in distinctive red, white and blue packets. Harissa, the red chilli sauce, can also be bought ready-made in cans or tubes.

50g/2oz dried chickpeas (*pois chiches*)
   or 1 (400g/14oz) can
2 tablespoons olive oil
1kg/2lb neck of lamb
2 large onions, skinned and chopped
2 turnips, peeled and quartered
2 carrots, peeled and sliced
a few saffron strands or 2 teaspoons
   ground turmeric
salt and freshly ground pepper
4 chicken joints (breast or leg), skinned
2 courgettes, chopped
125g/4½ oz broad beans (canned if
   necessary)
2 tomatoes, skinned and chopped
For the couscous
75g/3oz raisins
500g/1lb easy-cook couscous
25g/1oz butter or 1 tablespoon oil
50g/2oz flaked almonds
harissa

Put the chickpeas to soak the night
before if you are using dried ones.

Heat the oil in a large, heavy
saucepan and brown the lamb lightly.
Add the chickpeas, onion, turnips and
carrots and cover generously with
water. Bring to the boil and add the
pounded saffron or turmeric with
seasoning. Simmer, skimming the
top from time to time if necessary to
remove any scum. After 30 minutes,
put the chicken joints into the broth,
adding more water if necessary to cover
them. Bring back to the boil; cook for a
further 30 minutes.

Meanwhile, prepare the couscous:
take a ladleful of the broth and pour
it over the raisins to plump them up.
Measure out the couscous in cupfuls
and put it in a bowl. Add exactly the
same amount of boiling water by
volume – so if you use four cups of
couscous, add four cups of water.
Stir in the butter or oil with a fork
and leave for 15 minutes for the
grains to swell.

Then stir in the drained plumped
raisins and almonds. Add the
courgettes, broad beans and tomatoes
to the stew and bring back to the boil.
Fluff the grains of couscous with a
fork. Ladle them into a sieve or fine
colander (line one with scalded muslin
if necessary) and sit it in the top of the
saucepan, wrapping a folded tea towel
under the rim if necessary to stop it
dipping into the liquid. Cook for a
further 30 minutes. (Alternatively,
simply heat the couscous gently in a
saucepan, but the end result will not be
so fluffy.)

To serve, offer around the couscous
(which is eaten like rice) and the stew
separately, then pass the *harissa*. The
latter is extremely peppery and should
be added by each person, drop by
drop, to their stew until it is fiery
enough for their taste.

BOEUF BOURGUIGNON
BEEF IN RED WINE

SERVES FOUR

A signature recipe from Burgundy, for ultimate authenticity you should use Charolais beef and red burgundy wine (but not your best Romanée-Conti!). The mushrooms and onions should always be added near to the end of cooking.

1kg/2lb braising steak
25g/1oz flour
salt and freshly ground pepper
150g/5oz belly pork
1 shallot, chopped
1 onion, sliced
1 clove garlic, skinned and sliced
125ml/4fl oz brandy (optional)
500ml/17fl oz red burgundy
175ml/6fl oz beef stock
bouquet garni
25g/1oz butter
16 baby onions, peeled
16 button mushrooms, trimmed

Cut the steak into generous chunks and toss in flour seasoned with salt and pepper. Cut the pork into matchsticks and sauté in its own fat in a large, heavy flameproof casserole with a tight-fitting lid. Add the steak and brown it, then add the shallot, onion and garlic and let them soften but not burn. If you wish, add the brandy and set alight. Add the wine, stock and *bouquet garni*. Cover the pan and simmer very gently for 2½ hours.

The finest beef goes into a classic boeuf bourguignon.

Melt the butter in a frying pan and brown the baby onions and mushrooms, then add to the casserole. Cook for a further 20 minutes and serve. Chunks of crusty baguette and a green salad are all you need to mop up the delicious juices.

POULET À L'ESTRAGON
CHICKEN WITH TARRAGON

SERVES FOUR

This simple dish, which comes from the Lyonnais, is basically roast chicken – but vive la différence*! If the chicken comes without giblets, use a chicken stock cube to flavour the sauce. And if you want a richer version, stir a tablespoonful of thick cream into the gravy before serving.*

50g/2oz butter

3 tablespoons chopped fresh
  tarragon

1.5kg/3lb free-range (*fermier*) chicken
  with giblets

salt and freshly ground black pepper

2 tablespoons butter or oil, for
  cooking

Set the oven at 180°C, 350°F, gas 4.
Soften the 50g/2oz piece of butter and
pound it with the tarragon using a
pestle and mortar or with the back of
a metal spoon. Remove the giblets
from the chicken. Working your fingers
gently under the skin of the chicken
breast and lifting it as you go, spread
a layer of the tarragon mix over the
flesh. If there is any of the mixture
left over, put the rest inside the
chicken for extra flavour.

Cover the breast of the bird with foil.
Melt the 2 tablespoons butter or oil in
a baking tin and put in the bird. Roast
for one hour, removing the foil towards
the end so that the breast turns
golden brown.

Meanwhile, to make the stock, place
the giblets from the bird with 300ml/
½ pint water in a saucepan. Simmer
until the liquid is reduced by half. When
the chicken is done, remove it from
the pan, tipping the bird so that the
tarragon-flavoured juices run into the
pan. Pour in the strained giblet stock and
bring to the boil. Strain again and serve
with the bird.

Note. To check that the chicken is
cooked, pierce the meat at the thickest
part (behind the thighs) with the point
of a knife. If the juices run clear and
there are no signs of pink flesh, the
bird is cooked; if there is any blood or
pink meat visible, then cook the
chicken a little longer.

It is a good idea to check the bird
about three-quarters of the way through
cooking, particularly if you are using an
oven that is unfamiliar, as overcooked
chicken is disappointing.

*Chicken and tarragon are a match made
in heaven.*

CÔTE DE PORC NORMANDE
PORK WITH CIDER AND CALVADOS

SERVES FOUR

A quick pork dish from Normandy, which makes good use of the produce of the Normandy countryside – Calvados and cider. You can also stir in cream at the last minute to make an even more delicious dish. In this recipe the chops are fried, but they could equally well be grilled or baked in the oven, provided you are able to catch the juices to use them for the sauce. If grilling or baking, the apples can be cooked with the chops. Use shallots rather than onions if you can, as they give a more delicate flavour.

1 large clove garlic skinned and halved
4 pork chops
4 shallots or one large onion, skinned and finely chopped
75g/3oz butter
salt and freshly ground black pepper
2 large cooking apples
300ml/½ pint cider
2 tablespoons Calvados

Rub the cut clove of garlic over both sides of the pork chops. Cook the shallots or onion in 50g/2oz of the butter in a frying pan until softened. Add the chops and brown on each side. Season, then lower the heat, cover and cook until the chops are tender – about 20 minutes or more, according to their size.

Meanwhile core, but do not peel, the cooking apples, then cut them into thick rings. Poach them in the remaining butter in a separate pan.

Once the pork is cooked, lift out the chops and keep them warm while you prepare the sauce. Pour the cider into the frying pan and bring it to the boil, stirring in the juices from the meat and the shallots. Let it bubble fast to reduce it a little and thicken it slightly. Add the Calvados and bring back to the boil. Pour the sauce over the chops and serve, together with the apple rings.

LAPIN À LA DIJONNAISE
RABBIT IN MUSTARD SAUCE

SERVES FOUR

Roast rabbit tends to be rather dry, so anoint it with butter first, then top it with foil. You must use real Dijon mustard, which is readily available. The more fiery English version would make this recipe unpalatable. Traditionally, the rabbit is cooked whole, but you could joint it, reducing the baking time to 40 minutes. If you do not like rabbit, try substituting chicken instead, or pork chops, but leave out the marinade.

1 oven-ready rabbit
250ml/8fl oz wine vinegar

50g/2oz butter
1 small pot Dijon mustard
2 tablespoons oil
175ml/6fl oz *crème fraîche* or double
cream

Place the rabbit in a small oven dish,
pour over the vinegar and leave overnight
to marinate, turning it from time to time,
initially. This helps to make the flesh
tastier and more tender.

Set the oven at 190°C, 375°F, gas
mark 5. Drain the rabbit, pat it dry, then
smear it with the butter. Coat it liberally
with mustard and place it whole in a
baking dish with the oil. Cover the
rabbit with a piece of foil to stop it
becoming too dry. Roast for about an
hour (according to size); to test
whether it is cooked, spike with a sharp
knife to check that the juices are no
longer pink.

Remove the rabbit when it is cooked,
and put it on one side and keep warm.
Drain off some of the fat if there seems
to be too much, then stir the remainder,
scraping up the juices from the bottom
of the pan. Spoon in the *crème fraîche*
or cream over a very low heat. Take
care not to boil it or it may curdle.
Check the sauce for flavour, adding
more mustard if necessary. Pour over
the rabbit and serve.

TARTE AU CITRON
LEMON FLAN

SERVES SIX TO EIGHT
*French rich shortcrust pastry (pâte
sablée) is sweeter and more substantial
than shortcrust but you could substitute
the latter. The filling is pleasantly sharp.*

For the pastry
200g/7oz plain flour
pinch of salt
1 tablespoon caster sugar
125g/4½oz butter
1 egg
For the filling
5 eggs
125g/4½oz caster sugar
75g/3oz butter, melted
**finely grated rind of 2 lemons and juice
of 4 lemons**

Set the oven at 180°C, 350°F, gas 4.
For the pastry, sift the flour into a bowl
with the salt and sugar. Cut the butter
into small pieces and mix with a fork
until it looks like fine breadcrumbs. Beat
the egg with 2 tablespoons cold water
and work into the mixture, adding more
water if necessary. Work the pastry
into a ball, then roll it out and line a
25cm/10in flan tin. For the filling, whisk
the eggs and sugar together until fluffy.
Add the melted butter, lemon rind and
lemon juice. Pour into the flan case.
Bake for 35–40 minutes until the pastry
is golden and the filling set.

CLAFOUTIS
BAKED CHERRY PUDDING

SERVES SIX

This is a classic French dessert that comes from the Limousin. You can use canned cherries if fresh ones are not in season, or may substitute apples. This batter tart behaves like a Yorkshire pudding in that it puffs up, then sinks. It can be served hot, cold or just lukewarm, cut into wedges. Using unstoned cherries adds flavour – but it's advisable to warn your guests first!

25g/1oz butter, for greasing
125g/4½oz plain flour
pinch of salt
100g/4oz caster sugar
2 eggs
175ml/6fl oz milk
1 tablespoon dark rum (optional)
500g/1lb black cherries, unstoned

Set the oven at 180°C, 350°F, gas 4. Butter a 20cm/8in shallow baking tin (best) or flan dish (a loose-bottomed flan tin will leak) and put it in the oven to heat.

Put the flour, salt and half the sugar into a bowl. Beat the eggs, one at a time, and add to the mixture. Then, slowly, add the milk, beating it to a smooth batter. Alternatively, you can use a blender for this process. Next stir in the rum. Leave the mixture on one side and let it rest for about 10 minutes or so.

Take the tin from the oven, pour in the mixture and spoon in the fruit. Bake for 45 minutes to one hour. To test if the *clafoutis* is ready, pierce it with the point of a metal skewer; the skewer should come out clean. Remove from the oven, turn out the *clafoutis* and dust it with the rest of the sugar.

Tasty clafoutis is a great end to a meal.

Practical Information

Wherever you buy your produce, a little bit of the French language will go a long way.

Essentials for Travellers

SELF CATERING

If you are renting a *gîte* or a villa, it pays to take a small survival kit with you. For even though all officially registered *gîtes* will be well stocked, many villa owners assume that you are going to eat out, and although there may be generous amounts of crockery, the gadgets may be on the mean side. You are unlikely to find a kettle in your kitchen or teacups and saucers either. Bring your own tea, too. In many places, the cooker works off butane gas bottles, so it is as well to note where the nearest supplier is – usually the local garage.

WHAT TO BRING HOME

When buying food abroad do not flout the regulations and restrictions on the type and quantity of goods to bring home and avoid at all costs breaking common sense hygiene practices simply to transport a delicacy that may well go off after a long warm car journey. On the other hand, some canned items are well worth stowing in the boot of the car. Chestnut purée and whole chestnuts in cans are a fraction of the price you would pay at home, as are coffee beans. Canned *petits pois* with baby onions are delicious, as is canned *cassoulet*. Unusual *confitures* (jams) made from esoteric fruits such as greengages or bilberries make a good souvenir, as do olives, olive oil and walnut oil. Canned and bottled sauces such as *aïoli*, *rouille* and Hollandaise are also worth considering bringing home, as are pâtés preserved in jars which last a long time.

CURRENCY

The euro is the official currency of France. Euro bank notes and coins were introduced in January 2002.

Euro bank notes are in denominations of 5, 10, 20, 50, 100, 200 and 500 euros and coins come in 1, 2, 5,10, 20 and 50 cents and 1 and 2 euros. Euro traveller's cheques are widely accepted as are all major credit cards.

TIGHT BUDGET

Shopping in a supermarket for groceries means that you can tot up how much you are spending before you reach the check-out. Supermarket prices are cheaper, and a credit or debit card with chip-and-pin is a normal method of payment. Markets in France offer the best bargains – though the price difference is not so marked as in some places, because the French always go for quality. Do not be afraid to pick out just one aubergine (eggplant), or whatever, if that is what you need – the stall holder will not mind.

Equally, it is possible to ask for half a *baguette* from a *boulangerie* if that is all you need. Although the price of bread is likely to be the least of your worries, stale loaves can be revived if you sprinkle them with water and pop them in the oven, and toasted slices of yesterday's bread are perfectly acceptable for breakfast. Ready-made dishes from the take-away may look enticing but they are often pricey.

Meat is generally very expensive in France, so use it sparingly in dishes with plenty of vegetables added. Vegetables in season are very cheap, and can be exciting if you make them up into dishes such as *ratatouille* (see recipe, page 137); so a switch to a mainly vegetarian menu will save cash. Protein can be supplied by adding pulses such as some of the infinite variety of dried haricot beans, or chickpeas (*poischiches*).

The enticing look of the vegetables on sale may well inspire you to make some inexpensive filling soups, which are wonderful at midday, especially if the weather is chilly. In summer, tomatoes are very cheap, and they may be used to make an excellent salad – good for lunch with plenty of bread – or a wonderful fresh soup.

Eggs are also economical and can often be bought direct from farms. A hearty omelette will be nourishing and filling. Look for the words '*élevé en plein air*' if you prefer free-range eggs (or poultry). If you keep away from the more esoteric cheeses, this is another cheap way to eat. Fruit is an inexpensive item, too, and is often sold by the tray – if you are a large group this works out as an economical way to buy.

On the drinks front, a *Cave Co-opérative* will give you the best wine for your money. Check out the price of beer, on the other hand, before you buy, as it can be relatively expensive since much of it is imported.

SPECIAL EVENTS

France has a fair number of public holidays. In fact, there are certain times of the year when the country comes to a virtual stand-still – apart from the ubiquitous *boulangeries* (bakers) and the restaurants, which will be packed out with French families. The holidays to note are Easter Monday, Ascension Day and Whit Monday, all moveable dates according to the year's calendar, then May Day (1 May) and Victory Day (8 May). Bastille Day is celebrated on 14 July, and Assumption Day on 15 August. All Saints Day, 1 November, is a big, if rather sombre, event. Armistice Day is commemorated on 11 November with all the fervour of a country that suffered enemy occupation.

There are also likely to be local celebrations from time to time. The best way to find out about these is to enquire at the *Syndicat d'Initiative,* the tourist office. Most issue a calendar of events and can also recommend places to visit, give bus times and so on.

There are many food festivals worth seeing – the pink garlic festival at Lautrec, in the Tarn, in August, is one. There are fig auctions at St-Vaast-la-Hague, Normandy, in October and a strawberry feast in Plougastel, Brittany, in June. In August there is a grape festival in Sancerre, Loire. Wine festivals abound and, apart from the great November auctions at Beaune, Sancerre has a wine fair in June, and there is a national fair in August, as well as many others.

CUSTOMS

YES

From another EU country for personal use (guidelines):

3,200 cigarettes, 200 cigars, 3kg of tobacco
10 litres of spirits (over 22%)
20 litres of aperitifs
90 litres of wine, of which 60 litres can be sparkling wine
110 litres of beer

From a non-EU country for your personal use, the allowances are:

200 cigarettes OR
50 cigars OR 250 grams of tobacco
1 litre of spirits (over 22%) OR
2 litres of intermediary products (eg sherry) and sparkling wine
2 litres of still wine
50 grams of perfume
0.25 litres of eau de toilette
The value limit for goods is 175 euros.

Travellers under 17 years of age are not entitled to the tobacco and alcohol allowances.

NO

Drugs, firearms, ammunition, offensive weapons, obscene material, unlicensed animals.

Useful Words and Phrases

PRONUNCIATION

Vowels

■ *ai, e, ei, é,* are mostly pronounced like 'e' in 'Terry'. At the end of words, *é, ez, er, et* are usually spoken like the 'ay' in 'say'.

■ In some words, *e* is pronounced like 'e' in 'th<u>e</u>' (this is written as 'eu' in the pronunciation guides).

■ *a* is pronounced like 'a' in 'past', but is rather shorter.

■ *i* is pronounced like 'ee' in 'sheep' but is shorter.

■ *o* is pronounced like 'o' in 'hot' or 'ow' in 'low' (these appear as 'o' and 'oh' respectively in the pronunciation guides).

■ *ou* is pronounced like 'oo' in 'boot'.

■ *u* has no English equivalent. To practise the sound say: ooooo with rounded lips, then try to say eeeee without unrounding the lips (this sound is written as 'ew' in the pronunciation guides).

Nasal vowels

These have no equivalent in English. They are pronounced by shutting the mouth to the nose while pronouncing the vowel. You do not pronounce the 'n' (to indicate this the 'n' appears as N in the pronunciation guides).

■ Thus: *an, en* are pronounced 'ahN'; *on* as 'awN': *ain, ein, in* as 'aN' (the 'a' as in 'cat'); *un* as 'uN', eg, *un bon vin blanc* – uN bawN vaN blahN.

Consonants

Mostly like their equivalent in English, except:

■ *ch* is pronounced 'sh'.

■ *j* and *g* before *e* and *I* are pronounced like 's' in 'usual' (this appears as zh in the pronunciation guides).

■ *r* is strongly pronounced at the back of the throat. It appears as 'R' in the pronunciation guides.

■ *gn* is like 'ni' in 'onion'.

■ *ill* and *ilw* are pronounced with a 'y' sound as in 'beyond'. Consonants at the end of a word are mostly not pronounced.

HELPFUL PHRASES

I don't understand Je ne comprends pas *zheun kawNprahNpa*

Can you repeat that, please?
Voulez-vous bien répéter cela s'il vous plaît? *voolay voo byaN Repetay seula, seel voo pleh?*

Please speak more slowly S'il vous plaît parlez plus lentement *seel voo pleh paRlay plew lahNteumahN*

Please write it down Je vous prie de l'écrire *zheu voo pRee deu lekReeR*

Do you speak English? Vous parlez anglais? *voo paRlay ahNgleh?*

Is there anyone who speaks...? Y a-t'l quelqu'un qui parle...? *eeyateel kellkuN key pahle?*

QUESTIONS AND ANSWERS

What? Quoi? *kwa?*

When? Quand? *kahn?*

Why? Pourquoi? *pooRkwa?*

Which? Lequel?/Laquelle? *leukell/lakell?*

How long? Combien de temps? *kombeeaN deu tahN?*

How much? Combien? *kombeeyaN?*

I don't know Je ne sais pas *zheun seh pa*

NUMERALS

1	un	*uN*
2	deux	*deuh*
3	trois	*tRwa*
4	quatre	*katR*
5	cinq	*sanK*
6	six	*seess*
7	sept	*set*
8	huit	*weet*
9	neuf	*neuf*
10	dix	*deess*
11	onze	*awNz*
12	douze	*dooz*
15	quinze	*kaNz*
20	vingt	*vaN*
25	vingt-cinq	*vaNsaNk*
30	trente	*tRahNt*
40	quarante	*kaRahNt*
50	cinquante	*saNkahNt*
60	soixante	*swasshNt*
70	soixante-dix	*swassahNt deess*
80	quatre-vingt	*katRewvaN*
90	quatre-vingt-dix	*katrewvaN deess*
100	cent	*sahN*
200	deux cents	*deuh sahN*
300	trois cents	*tRwa sahN*
400	quatre cents	*katR sahN*
500	cinq cents	*sanK sahN*
600	six cents	*seess sahN*
700	sept cents	*set sahN*
800	huit cents	*weet sahN*
900	neuf cents	*neuf sahN*
1000	mille	*meell*
2000	deux mille	*deuh meell*

GREETINGS

Yes/no Oui/non *wee/nawN*

Please S'il vous plaît *seel voo pleh*

Thank you (very much) Merci (beaucoup) *meRsee (bokoo)*

You're welcome Je vous en prie *zheu voos oN pree*

Hello/goodbye Bonjour/au revoir *bawNzhooR/oRvwaR*

Where are you from? D'où venez-vous? *Doo veunay voo?*

How are you? Comment ça va? *kommahN sa va?*

Well, and you? Je vais bien, et vous? *zheu vay beeaN, ay voo?*

Delighted to meet you Enchanté *ahNshahNtay*

This is my wife (husband) Voici ma femme (mon mari) *vwassee ma famm (mawn maRee)*

Good morning Bonjour *bawNzhooR*

Good evening (and good night) Bonsoir *bawNswaR*

Good night Bonne nuit *bon nwee*

Tomorrow Demain *deumaN*

See you later À tout à l'heure *a too ta leur*

My name is... Je m'appelle... *zheu mappell...*

Have a good trip Je vous souhaite bon voyage *zheu voo sooette boN voyahje*

DIFFICULTIES

Excuse me Pardon! *PaRdawN!*

I'm sorry Excusez-moi *exkewzay mwa*

Is it far? (near?) C'est loin (tout près)? *seh lwaN (too pReh)?*

Can you help me? Pouvez-vous m'aider *poovay voo meday?*

Where are the toilets? Où sont les WC? *oo sawN leh doobleuvayssay?*

They are over there Elles sont là-bas *ellsoN labbah*

Could I use your phone/mobile? Puis-je utiliser votre téléphone/portable? *pweezheu youtilleezay vottreu taylayfoN?/portarb?*

I've lost my purse/wallet J'ai perdu mon porte-monnaie/portefeuille *zhay pairdew moN portermonnay/porterfur-yer*

Does it bother you if I smoke? Cela vous dèrangerait si je fume? *seula voo dayrahzheray see zheu fewme?*

MONEY

I would like to change these traveller's cheques Je voudrais changer ces travellers *zheu voodReh shahNzhay seh tRavellaiR*

Can I pay with this credit card? Je peux payer avec cette carte? *zheu peuh pahyay avek set kaRt?*

What time does the bank open? La banque s'ouvre à quelle heure? *la bahNk soovR a kell euR?*

What's the exchange rate? Quel est le taux de change? *kell ay le toe de shahNje?*

GOING SHOPPING

What day is the market? Quel jour a lieu le marché?
kell zhur uh leeyja le marshay?

What time do the shops open?
Les magasins s'ouvrent à quelle heure?
leh magazaN soovR a kel euR?

Are they open on Sundays?
Ils sont ouverts le dimanche?
eel sawN toovaiR ley deemahNsh?

What time do the shops close?
Les magasins se ferment à quelle heur?
leh magazaN seu feRm ta kel euR?

Is there a supermarket nearby?
Y a-t-il un supermarché près d'ici?
Ee ateel uN sewpeRmaRshay pReh deesee?

I want to buy... Je veux acheter...
zheu veuh ashtay...

I would like... J'aimerais... *zhemReh...*

Do you have...? Avez-vous...?
Avay voo...?

A packet of... Un paquet de...
uN pakeh deu...

A slice of meat Une tranche de viande
ewn tRahNsh deu vyahNd

I want fish for soup Je voudrais du poisson pour faire de la soupe
zheu voodray dew pwoissoN fair de la soope

Please clean them Pouvez-vous les vider
poovay voo lay veeday

Without heads and filleted Sans la tête ni les arrêtes *soN la tett knee layzarrette*

Do you have any cold meats? Avez vous de la viande froide?
avay voo deu la veeond frwudde?

Bigger, smaller Plus grand/plus petit
plew gRahn, plew peutee

For baking Pour cuire au four
poor qweer ohfoor

Can I help myself? Je peux me servir?
Zheu peuh meu seRveeR?

Don't touch! Ne touchez-pas!
neu tooshay pa!

Anything else? Et après? *eh apReh?*

That's it (no more) C'est tout *seh too*

How much is it? C'est combien?
seh kawNbyaN?

Go to the cash desk (till) Passez à la caisse *passay a la kehss*

TIME

Early/late Tôt/tard *toh/taR*

Sometimes Quelquefois *kelkeufwa*

In ... minutes Dans ... minutes *doN ... mihnewts*

What is the time? Quelle heure est-il? *kell euR eteel?*

After/before Après/avant *appray/avvoN*

WEIGHTS AND MEASURES

1kg un kilo *uN keeloh*

2kg deux kilos *deuh keeloh*

100g cent grammes
sahN gRamm

200g deux cent grammes
deuh sahN gRamm

1 litre un litre *uN leetR*

¾ trois quarts de... *tRwa kaR deu...*

½ un demi... *uN deumee...*

¼ un quart de... *uN kaR deu...*

a portion of une portion de...
ewn poRsyawn deu...

a cup une tasse... *ewn tass...*

a slice of une tranche de...
ewn tRahNsh deu...

a piece of un morceau de...
uN moRsoh deu...

twice that deux frois cela
deux fwa seula

a dozen une douzaine *ewn doozehn*

AT THE RESTAURANT

What time do you serve meals?
À quelle heure servez-vous les repas?
a kel euR seRvay voo leh Reupa?

I would like to book a table for four
Je voudrais réserver une table pour
quatre *zheu voodReh ReseRvay ewn
tableu pooR katR*

Is there a car park? Y a-t-il un parking?
ee ateel uN paRkeeng?

The menu please Le menu, s'il vous
plaît *le meunew seel voo pleh*

Dish of the day Le plat du jour
leu pla dew zhooR

First course Premier plat
pReumyay pla

Starter Entrée *ahNtray*

How is it cooked? C'est préparé
comment? *seh pRepaRay kommahN?*

What do you recommend? Que recom-
mandez-vous? *keu Reukommahnday voo?*

What is this, that? Qu'est-ce que c'est?
keskeusseh

A small portion Une petite portion
ewn peuteet poRsyawN

May I change my order? Je peux
changer la commande?
zheu peuh shahNzay la kommahNd?

Can we have some more bread?
Encore un peu de pain s'il vous plaît?
ahNkoR uN peu paN seel voo pleh?

A glass of white wine Un verre de blanc
uN vaiR deu blahN

A bottle of red wine Une bouteille de
rouge *ewn bootehy deu Roozh*

Would you like some coffee? Vous
prenez du café? *voo pReunay dew kafay?*

The bill L'addition *ladissyawn*

What is the charge? Combien je vous
dois? *kawNbyan zheu voo dwa?*

We enjoyed it, thank you Nous avons
trouvé très bon, merci *noo zavawN
tRoovay tReh bawN, meRsee*

Nothing else, thank you Rien d'autre,
merci *RyaN dohtR meRsee*

SPECIAL REQUIREMENTS

Please could you warm up the baby's bottle? S'il vous plaît, pouvez-vous chauffer le biberon? *seel voo pleh poovay voo shohffay leu beebRawn?*

May I have a glass of water, fruit juice? Je voudrais un verre d'eau, de jus de fruit? *zheu voodReh uN vaiR doh, deu jewd fRwee?*

Have you got a high-chair please?

Auriez-vous une chaise haute pour enfants? *oRyay voo ewn shehz oht pooR ahNFahn?*

A half portion of…, please Une demi-portion de… s'il vous plaît

ewn deumee poRsyawn deu… seel voo pleh

May I have a plate/spoon? Je voudrais une assiette/une cuillère?

zheu voodReh ewn assyett/ewn kweeyaiR?

Can you bring some serviettes, please? Apportez-nous des serviettes, s'il vous plaît?

appoRtaynoo deh seRvyett, seelvoo pleh?

I'm a vegetarian Je suis végétarien *zheu swee vezhetaRyan*

Is there meat in it? Ce plat contient de la viande? *Se pla kawNtyaN deu la vyahNd?*

I am a diabetic Je suis diabète *zheu zwee dyabeht*

I am allergic to shellfish Les crustacés ne me conviennent pas

leh kRewstassay neu meu kawNvyenn pa

I cannot eat flour (milk, sugar) Je ne digère pas la farine (le lait, le sucre)

zheu neu deezhaiR pa la faReen (leu leh, leu sewkR)

I am on a diet je suis au régime *zheu swee oh Rezheem*

Conversion Tables

NOTES ON USING THE RECIPES

Weights and measures are written in metric and imperial. Follow only one set of measures as they are not interchangeable.

FLUID CONVERSIONS

125ml/4fl oz	500ml/17fl oz
150ml/¼ pint (5fl oz)	600ml/1 pint (20fl oz)
175ml/6fl oz	750ml/1 ¼ pints
200ml/7fl oz	1 litre/1¾ pints
300ml/½ pint (10fl oz)	2 litres/3½ pints

WEIGHT CONVERSIONS

50g/2oz	175g/6oz	700g/1 ½lb
75g/3oz	250g/9oz	1kg/2lb
100g/4oz	350g/12oz	1.5kg/3lb
150g/5oz	500g/1lb	2kg/4lb

SPOON MEASURES

Spoon measures refer to the standard measuring spoons and all quantities are level unless otherwise stated. Do not use table cutlery and serving spoons as their capacity varies.

½ teaspoon – 2.5ml
1 teaspoon – 5ml
1 tablespoon – 15ml (3 teaspoons)

ABBREVIATIONS

Metric	Imperial
g – gram or gramme	oz – ounce
kg – kilogram	lb – pound
ml – millilitre	fl oz – fluid oz

OVEN TEMPERATURES

The following settings are used in the recipes in this book, providing centigrade, Fahrenheit and gas settings. However, cooking facilities in your holiday accommodation may be limited or oven settings may be different or unreliable, so watch dishes carefully when baking in an unfamiliar appliance.

110°C	225°F	gas ¼
120°C	250°F	gas ½
140°C	275°F	gas 1
150°C	300°F	gas 2
160°C	325°F	gas 3
180°C	350°F	gas 4
190°C	375°F	gas 5
200°C	400°F	gas 6
220°C	425°F	gas 7
230°C	450°F	gas 8
240°C	475°F	gas 9

AMERICAN MEASURES AND TERMS

Liquids:

	Imperial	American
	5fl oz	²/₃ cup
	8fl oz	1 cup
	10fl oz	1¼ cups
	16fl oz	2 cups
	20fl oz (1 pint)	2½ cups

Solids: Whole pounds and fractions of a pound are used for some ingredients, such as butter, vegetables and meat. Cup measures are used for storecupboard foods, such as flour, sugar and rice. Butter is also measured by sticks.

	Imperial	American
Butter	8oz	1 cup (2 sticks)
Cheese, grated, hard	4oz	1 cup
Flour	4oz	1 cup
Haricot beans, dried	6oz	1 cup
Mushrooms, sliced	8oz	2½ cups
Olives, whole	4oz	1 cup
Parmesan, grated	1oz	3 tablespoons, 2oz/¹/₃ cup
Peas, shelled	4oz	1 cup
Raisins	6oz	1 cup
Rice (uncooked)	8oz	1 cup

Acknowledgements

1 AA/R Strange; 5 AA/C Sawyer;
6 AA/C Sawyer; 7 AA/M Short;
11 AA/R Moore; 12 AA/R Moor;
15 AA; 18 AA/R Moore; 21 AA/J
Wyand; 24 AA/R Moore; 27 AA/J
A Tims; 31 AA/I Dawson; 32 Brand
X Pictures; 37 AA/C Sawyer; 38
AA/R Moore; 41 AA/C Sawyer; 44
AA/C Sawyer; 47 AA/C Sawyer; 50
AA/C Sawyer; 53 AA/W Voysey; 54
AA/C Sawyer; 59 AA/C Sawyer; 62
AA/C Sawyer; 68 AA/R Moore; 72
AA/C Sawyerl 75 AA/N Setchfield;
80 AA/C Sawyer; 83 AA/C Sawyer;
86 AA/C Sawyer; 87 AA/R Strange;
88 AA/A Baker; 89 AA/P Kenward;
91 AA/T Oliver; 92 AA/P Kenward;
96 AA/A Baker; 103 AA/R Moore;
104 AA/M Short; 107 AA/R Moore;
109 AA/P Kenward; 111 AA/N
Setchfield; 115 AA/C Sawyer; 117
AA/C Sawyer; 118 AA/J Wyand; 120
AA/C Sawyer; 121 AA/C Sawyer;
123 AA/C Sawyer; 126 AA/C
Sawyer; 131 AA/M Jourdan; 132
AA/E Meacher; 134 AA/J A Tims;
137 AA; 138 AA/B Bachman; 139
Stockbyte; 140 AA/E Meacher; 142
AA/C Sawyer; 143 AA/E Meacher;
146 AA/E Meacher; 147 AA/C
Sawyer